The
Acai Berry Miracle

The
Acai Berry
Miracle

60 BOWL AND SMOOTHIE RECIPES

Annie Willis

Racehorse Publishing

Introduction

Are you ready to look and feel better than you ever have? Acai is here to help! This miraculous little fruit is brimming with vitamins, minerals, and antioxidants that can help you strengthen your immune system, get glowing skin, fend off free radicals, protect your brain, lower your cholesterol, and fight inflammation. But acai really shines when you use it as the foundation for other fresh, nourishing ingredients. A single smoothie or bowl becomes a mouthwatering multivitamin.

The Acai Berry Miracle shows you how to use these combinations to unlock acai's full potential. You can balance your blood sugar, improve your digestion, protect your heart, enhance your eyesight, and even slim down with just a few small tweaks to your routine. And you'll start seeing the incredible benefits of acai blends immediately—they fill you up, boost your mood, and give you the energy you need to tackle your day.

When you're ready to harness the miracles of acai and take control of your health, you'll start with the 10-Day Acai-Powered Wellness Challenge. This isn't a diet or a detox. This is a fully flexible framework that empowers you to choose how you want to feel.

During your wellness challenge, you'll enjoy one smoothie and one bowl each day to let your body get used to superfood blends. You'll also develop a healthy routine that includes balanced meals, movement, and mindfulness. And you'll do it all *your way* so that those good habits stick. Eat the foods you like, choose movement that makes you happy, and find some time for rest and relaxation. Sound good? It gets better!

The Acai Berry Miracle offers you 60 delicious recipes full of amazing combinations like chocolate peanut butter and coconut-mango—all organized to help you feel your best. Whether you love a good vegan eatery or you hit the drive-thru every night, these acai smoothies and bowls will work for you. Plus, you'll learn how to make your own healthful blends using your favorite ingredients.

If you're ready to feel happier, healthier, and more energized, don't wait another minute! Discover how acai can help in *The Acai Berry Miracle*.

PART 1

The Powerful Acai Berry

Acai has become a mainstream flavor that's synonymous with wellness. You almost expect to see it listed (usually alongside blueberry) in healthy options like yogurts and teas. But you can also find it promising to imbue its mysterious powers of good health in everything from chocolates to energy drinks. This magical berry seems to have popped up overnight and taken over grocery stores everywhere.

But there's nothing mysterious or magical about acai—it's just a humble little fruit that's jam-packed with healthful vitamins, minerals, and antioxidants. Although it only made its way to the United States in the early 2000s, acai has been a nutritious staple of its native countries for centuries. To the generations who grew up with it, eating acai is like enjoying a handful of blueberries.

If you're in the States, though, you're not likely to find acai in your local produce aisle. Acai is highly perishable and must be processed and frozen within hours of picking. Unless you have a tropical greenhouse in your backyard, you're most likely to find acai as a frozen puree or freeze-dried powder.

No matter what form you find it in, acai will still deliver its miraculous nutritional benefits. You can enjoy more energy, a stronger immune system, better digestion, improved brain function, lower cholesterol, glowing skin, and more. Let acai help you take control of your health and get ready to feel amazing!

Acai 101

First things first—how on earth do you say it? Acai is pronounced ah-sigh-EE. This deep purple fruit is native to tropical Central and South America, and the name is a Portuguese adaptation of the indigenous word for it. (That's why you'll often see it written as *açaí*.) You'll find acai berries on the açaí palm, or *Euterpe oleracea*, a tree that can grow up to 100 feet tall, with leaves up to 10 feet long. The berries grow in clusters on dense branches beneath the leaves, with each branch bearing between 500 and 900 fruits.

But acai "berries" aren't berries at all—they're drupes (fruits that have pits, like cherries and apricots). Although they look like blueberries, the edible portion of acai is just a thin outer layer over a pit that generally takes up 80 percent of the fruit. And the taste is nothing like a sweet, juicy, ripe blueberry, either. Instead, it's often described as something between a blackberry and dark chocolate. (And if you think that sounds earthy and a little bitter, you're right. Often, you'll find this low-sugar fruit mixed with something sweeter.)

As you might imagine, harvesting acai berries from their giant palms is a challenge. For centuries, locals have been climbing the trees in bare feet, with no equipment, and harvesting 10-pound branches of berries by hand. And that's exactly how it's done today. Because acai is so highly perishable, it's quickly loaded into hand-woven baskets and transported by boats to processing plants. Within hours, the berries are washed, pureed, and frozen for packing and shipping all over the world.

Acai might be the newest member of the superfood group here in North America, but people in Central and South America have understood its powerful benefits since the beginning. From its legendary origins to its voyage north, acai's place in the superfood lineup has only become clearer and more compelling.

THE LEGEND OF IAÇÁ

As a staple of Brazil, the acai berry carries with it a long and storied history. *Acai* is a Portuguese adaptation of a Tupian word that means "fruit that cries." Although you might assume that this is due to acai's dark purple juice, local folklore tells a different tale—the story of a heartbroken mother whose tears brought acai to her people.

Legend has it that a severe drought threatened the survival of an Amazonian tribe at the mouth of the river near the modern-day city of Belém (in northeast Brazil). The resulting famine forced the village elders to make a hard choice. They decreed that, with hardly enough food and water for existing members, any newborn children would have to be sacrificed.

Little did the village's chief, Itaqui, expect that his own grandson would be the first to fall to that decree. Itaqui's daughter begged him to see reason. By the time she gave birth, the fields were green and the area's resources were recovering. But the chief was bound by the elders' wisdom. He sacrificed his grandson for the good of the tribe.

His grief-stricken daughter locked herself away and prayed to the gods for a way to end the sacrifices. After crying herself to sleep, the girl awoke to the cries of a child. She followed the sound to the base of a palm tree and found her own smiling son. Reaching to embrace him, she found her arms wrapped instead around the trunk of the tree. And there, at the base of the palm, she lost the will to live.

Itaqui found his daughter the next morning, her arms still wrapped around the tree and her beautiful, dark eyes fixed on a cluster of berries. The tribe gathered the berries, drank their dark juice, and realized that this fruit was the answer to all their prayers. Chief Itaqui thanked the gods for allowing him to end the sacrifices and declared that the berries would honor his daughter. He reversed the letters of her name—Iaçá—and called them açaí.

FROM SAVORY TO SWEET

Acai has always been an incredibly important source of food and nutrition for the indigenous populations of the Amazon area, and it still is today. One study found that the fruit makes up 42 percent of the average diet in the Brazilian Amazon. Although we think of acai in terms of berry-filled smoothies and protein-packed breakfast bowls, in the Amazon, you'll find it featured in savory meals alongside things like fish and cassava root.

It wasn't until the 1980s that acai became the star of sweet treats, thanks to one entrepreneurial family. Famous for their Brazilian jiujitsu gyms, the Gracies family viewed acai as the perfect nutritional complement to their training programs. But they knew that not everyone enjoyed acai's earthy flavor. Thankfully, the frozen puree being shipped out of Brazil made the perfect base for smoothies full of sweeter ingredients.

The Gracies began mixing acai with bananas and guarana (a sweet Brazilian berry that's full of caffeine) and serving the thick smoothies to their athletes. As the bowls became more and more popular, the Gracies seized on the opportunity to open a shop. And then another. And another. Before long, acai bars were popping up all over Brazil.

That's where American brothers Ryan and Jeremy Black and their friend Edmund Nichols had their first bowls, and it was love at first taste. By the end of their trip, they were determined to bring acai home to the United States. They started a company called Sambazon—the first to process and import frozen acai to the US, and now the brand you're most likely to find in your freezer section.

It's also thanks to this traveling trio that you can find acai bowls at cafes and smoothie shops around the country. They started out selling the concept from store to store in their native southern California before moving on to Miami and New York City. Little by little, acai picked up steam and became the superfood that's sweeping the nation.

A SUSTAINABLE SUPERFOOD

Acai is a sustainable crop for the region, having always been harvested by hand and sold locally at markets and in private homes. In addition to the fruit, people use the leaves of the palm trees to make hats, masks, baskets, brooms, and roof thatch. And although most trees are left standing to produce fruit, they can also be cut down to make pest-resistant building material. Even the large pits of the fruit are used in organic soil and livestock feed.

Understanding the history and importance of acai in its native Brazil, the Sambazon team is dedicated to supporting the area with sustainable practices. They say the business has a "triple bottom line": people, planet, and prosperity. Ryan Black explains, "We're trying to use our business to combat challenges like poverty, malnutrition, inequality, and deforestation."

So far, they have supported 20,000 family farmers; have built and renovated area health centers, schools, and community centers; and have helped protect 2.5 million acres of rainforest and the native species that inhabit it. And in doing all of that, they've helped set the tone for the whole industry. In other words, you can feel as good about buying acai as you do about eating it.

The Many Benefits of Acai

With a powerful combination of antioxidants, vitamins, minerals, and other nutrients, acai earns the title of "superfood." Compare the fruit to another well-known superfood—blueberries—and you'll find that acai has more antioxidants, protein, calcium, iron, and vitamins A and C, plus acai is higher in healthy fats and lower in sugar. And with credentials like that, it's no wonder acai has such a tremendous effect on your health. But what exactly makes acai so miraculous? Read on to discover how each of acai's nutritional components can help you lower your blood pressure, cholesterol, and blood sugar, boost your immune system and brain function; stop the signs of aging in their tracks; and even help protect you from chronic illness and cancer!

ANTIOXIDANTS AND PHYTONUTRIENTS

By now, you probably know that antioxidants are good for you because they fight free radicals, but you might not know what that means. In short, it means that antioxidants keep your cells healthy.

Free radicals are unstable atoms that attach to healthy cells and cause oxidative damage or stress. And that damage can lead to little things, like wrinkles, or big things, like the inflammation associated with chronic illness and certain types of cancer. Your body naturally fights free radicals, but it needs all the help it can get. In addition to your body making them, free radicals come from exposure to toxins, such as pollution or cigarette smoke.

Antioxidants like the ones found in acai bind to free radicals so that they're no longer free to bind to healthy cells and cause problems. By simply digesting acai and other antioxidant-rich foods, you release these helpful nutrients into your bloodstream to uncover any lurking free radicals. And antioxidants alone can do you so much good!

It's thanks to its antioxidants that acai has been shown to stop cancer cells from forming and spreading. Plus, the fruit is neuroprotective because antioxidants counteract the damaging effects of inflammation and oxidation in brain cells. Studies also show that it helps improve memory and allows the brain to clean up toxic cells and make way for new nerves. In other words, the antioxidants in acai help your brain fire on all cylinders. And you can find them hiding in plain sight among several nutrients, including vitamins C and E, polyphenols, and phytonutrients like anthocyanins.

ANTHOCYANINS AND OTHER FLAVONOIDS
If you've ever mentioned the antioxidants in wine as an excuse to pour yourself another glass, then you're already familiar with anthocyanins. They're the antioxidants that give red wine (and acai) its coloring and its reputation for supporting good health.

Although all twelve of the flavonoids in acai have antioxidant effects, anthocyanins may be the most beneficial. Their anti-inflammatory properties may help ease symptoms of chronic illness, protect against neurogenerative diseases, improve blood flow to the brain, and enhance your memory. Anthocyanins have also been shown to reduce the risk of heart attack by 32 percent in young and middle-age women when consumed regularly.

Plus, anthocyanins have powerful cancer-fighting effects. Anthocyanins have been shown to activate detoxifying enzymes, stop cancer from spreading, kill cancer cells, and even prevent cancer from forming entirely. So, you can feel good about that glass of wine, but you'll feel even better with a glass of acai, which contains up to 30 times the anthocyanins.

Fun fact: Like acai, cacao beans are rich in polyphenols, which may partially explain the similar flavor between the two. It definitely explains why both are heart healthy superfoods. Polyphenols are the largest group of phytochemicals found in plants. And like other phytochemicals, they may help combat the inflammation linked to heart disease and neurodegenerative illnesses. But that's not all—they've also been shown to improve digestion, balance blood sugar, and aid weight loss. Plus, the polyphenols in acai may help improve your blood flow by boosting nitric oxide in the endothelial cells that line the arteries and blood cells, and that relaxes the arteries and improves your blood pressure.

VITAMINS

You know you need vitamins. They energize you, strengthen your immune system, help your body heal, protect your heart, and so much more. But did you know that your body can't produce vitamins? In fact, the only way to get the vitamins you need is to consume them through nutrient-rich foods like acai. So when you combine acai with other nourishing ingredients in smoothies and bowls, you're actually creating a powerful (and delicious) multivitamin. Acai's contribution includes vitamins A, C, and E, as well as three different B vitamins.

VITAMIN A

The vitamin A you get from fruits and veggies comes from the antioxidant beta-carotene—the same eyesight-enhancing nutrient found in carrots. Vitamin A is also vital for immune and reproductive health, good skin, and cell growth. And one serving of acai contains 15 percent of the recommended daily value of vitamin A.

Although you can find plenty of fruits and veggies that are high in vitamin A, you won't find any with the healthy fats that acai contains. And it's those healthy fats that help your body absorb vitamin A and gain its benefits. (Of course, you can also top your acai bowl with yummy ingredients like avocado, almonds, dark chocolate, or chia seeds for an extra dose of healthy fats.)

VITAMIN C

Acai may not technically be a berry, but it carries the same amount of powerful vitamin C as its look-alike, the blueberry. And if you've ever reached for a glass of orange juice at the first sign of the sniffles, you already know the importance of vitamin C. Not only does it support your immune system, it also can protect your heart, prevent eye disease, fend off free radicals, and fight the signs of aging. Plus, it's essential for healing and the formation of blood vessels, cartilage, muscle, and collagen in bones. Want to maximize those benefits? Add other vitamin C–rich foods to your acai bowls, including citrus, kiwi, and, of course, blueberries.

VITAMIN E

Want a healthy immune system? Glowing skin? Good vision? Then you're going to need the antioxidant benefits found in vitamin E. And as an antioxidant, vitamin E can also help protect your cells against the oxidative stress that can lead to inflammatory illnesses like arthritis and serious conditions like Alzheimer's and cancer. That's why vitamin E supplements are so popular, but they can't provide the benefits of the naturally occurring antioxidants found in food. Like vitamin A, vitamin E is fat soluble, so make sure you eat your acai with foods full of healthy fats (like almonds or chia seeds) to help your body absorb the vitamin.

B VITAMINS

Have you ever noticed that B vitamins are listed on the ingredients label of nearly every energy drink? That's because they help the body convert food into energy, create new blood cells, and maintain healthy brain cells. In other words, B vitamins are essential for your energy levels and brain function. And acai happens to have a few of these superstars on its roster.

- **Vitamin B_1 (thiamine).** In addition to helping you convert food into energy, thiamine plays an important role in nerve, muscle, and heart function. It's also essential for glucose metabolism, which helps you balance your blood sugar and energy levels.
- **Vitamin B_2 (riboflavin).** With an extra boost of antioxidant properties, riboflavin prevents cell damage as well as helping your body produce red blood cells. Plus, a regular dose of vitamin B_2 has been shown to prevent cataracts and migraines.
- **Vitamin B_3 (niacin).** Niacin stands out among the B vitamins because every part of your body needs it to function properly. In the right amount, it may also help lower cholesterol, prevent heart disease, treat type 1 diabetes, protect skin cells, ease arthritis, and boost cognitive function. (Too much niacin can cause trouble, but it'd be very hard to get too much from food.)

MINERALS AND ELECTROLYTES

If you look at the ingredients list on the back of a bottle of multivitamins, you'll see more than just vitamins. Those other ingredients—calcium, iron, and zinc, for example—are minerals. They're essential nutrients that your body can't live without, responsible for things like keeping your bones strong, your brain functioning, and your heart healthy. Luckily, you can get plenty of them from the food you eat, including acai.

Several of the minerals that acai contains are also electrolytes, which are electrically charged minerals that help your body do things like make your heart beat (a muscle contraction) and help your blood clot. Calcium, magnesium, manganese, potassium, and phosphorus are all electrolytes. Not getting enough electrolytes can wreak havoc on your system, but don't reach for that sugary sports drink just yet! Barring illness, a balanced diet full of healthy veggies and fruits like acai should be all you need.

CALCIUM

Thinking about calcium might conjure up the image of a cold glass of milk, but plenty of fruits and veggies contain calcium. Blackberries and kiwifruit, for example. And, of course, acai. In addition to helping you strengthen your bones and teeth, calcium is an electrolyte that's essential for muscle contraction, nerve impulse transmission, and blood vessel function. If you're looking to add an extra dose of this mineral to your acai smoothies, blend in a handful of calcium-rich spinach. You won't be able to taste it, but it will do you a world of good.

CHROMIUM

Chromium sounds like something you'd find on a car rather than something you need to eat. But it's actually an essential trace mineral that can help improve insulin sensitivity and enhance protein, lipid, and carbohydrate metabolism.

COPPER

Copper is another trace mineral (a mineral you don't need a lot of) that affects a wide range of bodily functions. It plays a role in energy production, the formation of collagen, iron absorption and the creation of red blood cells, nerve cell maintenance, and immune health. Studies show that it may also protect you from arthritis, high blood pressure, high cholesterol, and osteoporosis.

IRON

This trace mineral couldn't be more important—it's a component of hemoglobin, a protein needed to transport oxygen from your lungs to the rest of your body. Iron also supports a healthy pregnancy, high energy, and athletic performance.

MANGANESE

Manganese is a little mineral that is involved in a lot of different processes. It supports strong bones, balanced blood sugar, blood clotting, and wound healing. Plus, it helps your body metabolize amino acids, cholesterol, glucose, and carbohydrates.

MAGNESIUM

Your body needs magnesium for more than 300 biochemical reactions, including the metabolism of food, synthesis of proteins and fatty acids, and the transmission of nerve impulses. Magnesium also supports a regular heartbeat, a healthy immune system, and strong bones, while regulating blood glucose levels and contributing to energy production. For a tasty, magnesium-rich boost, sprinkle a tablespoon or two of sunflower seeds on top of your acai smoothie or bowl.

POTASSIUM

Potassium can be a life saver—adequate potassium intake can reduce your overall risk of death by 20 percent, not to mention decreasing your risk of stroke, lowering your blood pressure, protecting your muscles and bones, and inhibiting kidney stones. But potassium's main jobs are regulating fluid balance and controlling the electrical activity of muscles, including the heart. Because potassium is a micromineral, you need more of it than other minerals. But by mixing a frozen banana into your acai smoothie or bowl, you'll be well on your way to consuming your recommended daily amount.

PHOSPHORUS

Like calcium, phosphorus builds strong bones and teeth. But it also makes proteins that grow and repair cells and tissues, aids muscle recovery after exercise, promotes healthy nerve function, manages the body's energy, and filters and removes waste from the kidneys. Plus, it's essential for making DNA and RNA. And it's easy to get enough phosphorus from food alone.

ZINC

Ever notice how many cold and flu medicines contain zinc? That's because zinc is vital to protecting your immune health by fighting off bacteria and viruses. Your body also uses zinc in the processes of DNA synthesis, digestion, wound healing, and metabolism. The next time you're feeling a little under the weather, whip up an acai bowl with other zinc-rich fruits, such as avocado, blackberries, pomegranate seeds, and kiwi slices.

AMINO ACIDS

You may remember from seventh-grade science class that "amino acids are the building blocks of protein." Your body needs twenty of them to grow and function properly, and acai happens to contain nineteen. Nine of these are essential to your health and can only come from food. These include:

- **Histidine.** Histidine is integral to growth, the creation of blood cells, tissue repair, protection of nerve cells, immunity, reproduction, and digestion.
- **Isoleucine.** Isoleucine is important for wound healing, immune function, blood sugar regulation, hormone production, hemoglobin production, and energy regulation.
- **Leucine.** Leucine is required for wound healing, growth, the repair of muscle and bone, and blood sugar regulation.
- **Lysine:** Lysine is key in energy production, immune function, building strong muscles and bones, recovery from injury, and regulating hormones, enzymes, and antibodies.
- **Methionine.** Methionine is crucial for good health, skin, and hair, as well as the proper absorption of selenium and zinc and the removal of heavy metals.
- **Phenylalanine.** Phenylalanine helps the body use the other amino acids as well as proteins and enzymes. It's also essential for certain brain functions.
- **Threonine.** Threonine is a component of tooth enamel, collagen, and elastin, so it's essential for healthy skin and teeth. It also helps with fat metabolism.
- **Tryptophan.** Tryptophan is a precursor of serotonin and melatonin, which together help regulate your appetite, sleep, mood, and pain.
- **Valine.** Valine helps stimulate muscle growth, coordination, and regeneration as well as energy, mental focus, and emotional well-being.

PLANT STEROLS

It's a good idea to watch your cholesterol at any age, but especially as you get older. The plant sterols you find in fruits like acai, veggies, and nuts can help with that. Plant sterols are naturally occurring cholesterol-like substances that trick your body into absorbing them instead of LDL (bad) cholesterol. Acai contains three: beta-sitosterol, campesterol, and stigmasterol. In addition to fighting high cholesterol and preventing heart disease, plant sterols may aid weight loss and even help prevent cancer. Plus, some skincare brands use plant sterols from acai (specifically beta-sitosterol) in their products to refresh and hydrate skin.

LOW SUGAR

Although naturally derived sugar from fruit is different from the added sugars you find in processed foods (fruit sugar metabolizes more slowly, so you don't have sugar crashes), you'll still want to be careful not to overdo it. Too much of a good thing can be a not-so-good thing. If acai is your foundation, you're off to a good start.

Acai berries have just 2 grams of natural sugar per serving. Compare that with a medium apple, which has 19 grams, or blueberries, which have 15 grams per serving. Just don't be tempted to overcompensate for the lack of sugar when building your smoothie bowls. Stick to unsweetened toppings and low-glycemic fruit, especially if your blood sugar level or weight loss is a concern.

HEALTHY FAT

Unlike most varieties of fruit, acai is full of the healthy fats that help lower blood sugar and bad cholesterol while boosting good cholesterol. These include omega-3, omega-6, and omega-9 fatty acids, the most important of which is omega-3. Because the body can't produce omega-3 fatty acids, it's important that you get enough through food (which most Westerners don't). Omega-3 fatty acids fight inflammation, strengthen bones, prevent asthma, keep skin hydrated, maintain mental health, and support a healthy heart, brain, and weight. To make sure you're getting enough of these healthy fats, add toppings like avocado and pumpkin seeds to your acai bowls.

DIETARY FIBER

Acai berries contain 2 grams of dietary fiber per serving, and that's all thanks to the skin of the fruit. Although 2 grams may not seem like much, it's 8 percent of your recommended daily value. Combine acai with other high-fiber ingredients, such as bananas, blueberries, and chia seeds, and you're well on your way to getting the fiber you need to feel full and ease your digestion, not to mention lower your cholesterol and balance your blood sugar. Plus, studies show that getting enough fiber is linked to a significantly lower risk of developing heart disease and a slower progression of the disease in people at high risk for it.

CALORIES

You might think that the fewer calories you consume, the better. But everyone needs a certain number of calories per day in order to function well and maintain his or her energy and good health. In other words, if you want to make it through the day, you're going to need some food in your stomach and calories in your system.

The number of calories you need to eat depends on several factors, including sex, age, weight, and general level of activity. (Talk to a healthcare professional to determine your ideal range.) But generally speaking, an adult female should consume 2,000 calories per day, and an adult male needs around 2,500. That's not an excuse to go out and grab a bacon cheeseburger, though. You want those calories to fuel you, not drain you.

If getting enough *healthy* calories is a problem for you, acai may be the answer. With about 80 calories per serving, it beats out other "high-calorie" fruits like dates and figs. Combine all three, and you have a tasty and filling acai bowl!

To Your Health!

All these incredible nutrients are packed into just 20 percent of each tiny "berry." And eating this delicious superfood benefits not only your health, but also the people and places that have been cultivating it for centuries. That's a wonderful win-win!

Now that you know what acai brings to the table, you're ready to learn how to make the most of it. Acai smoothies and bowls turn the fruits and veggies you already love into powerful tonics that can help you meet your health goals. In the next part, you'll discover where to find this miraculous fruit, how to prepare it, and—most importantly—how to blend it with other nutritional superstars to create the most flavorful and nourishing combinations.

Think it can't get any better? Wait until you've tried the 10-Day Acai-Powered Wellness Challenge (starting on page 45). This easy and flexible plan will give you the tools you need to feel better than you ever have!

PART 2

Making the Most of Your Acai

I deally, now that you know the wealth of nutrients that are magically packed into each little acai berry, you're excited to dive into some scrumptious acai smoothies and bowls. But, to get the most out of your acai, you'll need to learn a few basics. This chapter has everything you need to know to become a smoothie-bowl-making pro in no time! You'll learn where to find acai, how to prep your produce, what kind of equipment you'll need, and how to use it. Plus, you'll discover all the incredible benefits you can get from combining acai with powerful produce partners.

This chapter will set you up for the ultimate success during your 10-Day Acai-Powered Wellness Challenge. Not only will you go into your wellness journey knowing how to create incredible acai-powered smoothies and bowls, you'll also learn how to customize your recipes to your tastes and desired effects. Want an anti-aging boost? Add blueberries. Want your morning energy to last until the afternoon? Make sure you add some healthy protein, such as chopped nuts. Having all the information ensures that you hit the ground running on Day 1!

Acai in All Its Forms

As you learned in Part 1, fresh acai is hard to come by outside of the Brazilian Amazon. But that's a good thing! Using acai in its exported forms means that it's prepped and ready to go without you having to do a thing. If you had to use whole acai berries, you would need to wash and pit a lot of berries to get enough pulp for one smoothie. Instead, you'll just head to your local supermarket and pick up some frozen puree or powder.

FROZEN PUREE

Frozen puree is the most common form of acai, which is why you'll find it listed in all of this book's recipes. You're most likely to find it in the freezer section of your local grocery store, but you can also easily order it online from major retailers. And because acai has become so popular, you're likely to find quite the selection. In addition to pure, unsweetened acai, you can find acai blends with guarana (the original variety made popular by the Gracies), tropical fruits, berries, protein powder, and greens. Some of these are sweetened, and some aren't. But they all come in easy-to-grab pre-measured packets that you just open and squeeze into a blender.

One packet of frozen puree is a serving and can be used to create one to two smoothies or bowls. Start with one packet of pure, unsweetened acai puree per serving. Once you get the hang of things, you can tailor recipes to your tastes with more or less acai and try out other flavors and varieties.

FREEZE-DRIED POWDER

Depending on where you live, freeze-dried acai powder might be easier to find than frozen puree. It's also easy to order from major retailers and health-food markets online. When you search for this form of acai, you might also find powdered nutritional supplements that *contain* acai. Just make sure that what you're buying is 100 percent freeze-dried acai powder.

You're less likely to find sweetened varieties in powder form, but brands are starting to branch out in flavors. (One even offers acai powder pre-blended with cacao and goji berries.) For now, stick with the all-acai versions. The recipes in this book all use frozen puree to keep things simple. But if you want to use powder instead, just substitute two tablespoons of the powder for each packet of frozen puree.

ACAI JUICE

Because acai berries aren't readily available outside of the Amazon, you're not going to find fresh-pressed acai juice. What you see on supermarket shelves is juice made with frozen acai puree. Although you can find just-acai juice, you're more likely to find blends that contain acai. Either way, juices are often chock-full of added ingredients like preservatives and sweeteners, so be sure to read those labels. (And make sure you buy only pasteurized juice—unpasteurized juice can carry Chagas disease.)

Juices are a great way to pack even more acai goodness into your day. If you want to up the acai ante and add a bit more flavor to your smoothies and bowls, you can substitute any variety of acai juice for the liquid in your recipes. You can also freeze acai juice in an ice cube tray so that you always have it on hand to throw in a smoothie or bowl.

ACAI CAPSULES AND SUPPLEMENTS

Because acai is a powerful superfood, it was bound to end up in vitamins and supplements. These products usually contain freeze-dried acai powder. Not all of these are created equal, so read the ingredients lists carefully if you plan to purchase any. And remember that the FDA doesn't monitor health supplements, so you never can be sure what you're getting. While quality supplements are an easy way to consume acai, they're not the most nutritious or enjoyable. Stick to smoothies and bowls for the most comprehensive health benefits.

CLEAN

When you cook your produce, you're heating it to a temperature that destroys any harmful chemicals and bacteria. That's not the case with smoothies, so it's important to buy "clean" fruits and veggies. Choosing organic produce is first and foremost—these items are held to rigorous health and safety standards. From soil and water quality to pest-control methods, organic farmers must be meticulous. And that means you're getting the best of the best.

Studies show that organic produce contains more nutrients, lower amounts of toxic metals (which can be absorbed through the soil), and lower levels of pesticides than conventionally grown produce. In fact, organic farmers have to use natural methods to discourage pests. And that's good for you, because pesticides have been shown to cause fertility issues, respiratory illness, neurological disorders, and even certain types of cancer.

Don't let that scare you too much, though. There are plenty of fruits and veggies that are perfectly fine to eat regardless of whether they're grown organically. These belong to the Environmental Working Group's "Clean Fifteen" and include avocados, pineapples, papayas, kiwis, and cantaloupes. Bananas and most berries aren't in the top fifteen, but they're still considered very safe. The items you really want to buy organic are on the Environmental Working Group's "Dirty Dozen" list. These include strawberries, spinach and kale, nectarines and peaches, apples and pears, grapes, cherries, and celery.

FROZEN

Making your own acai-powered smoothies and bowls doesn't have to be time consuming. (Like you don't have enough to do without adding produce prep to your list!) Pre-packaged frozen fruit is a totally acceptable time-saver. Not only that, but it's usually cheaper than its fresh counterpart, and your local grocery store always has plenty of options available. Plus, it probably contains more nutrients than your grocery store's produce because it was cleaned, frozen, and packed at the peak of freshness. And if that's not enough, frozen fruit can also sit in your freezer for a year without spoiling. You're lucky if you get a week out of fresh berries, so using frozen berries means less food waste. One small word of caution: If you have any allergies, look carefully at your package of frozen fruit. Depending on where it was processed, it may have a cross-contamination warning.

PREPPING YOUR PRODUCE

Adding frozen acai puree to your blender is easy: just run the sealed packet under warm water or let it thaw for a minute before cutting it open and squeezing the acai into the blender. Depending on the type and size of your blender, you might also want to break the block of acai in half. Adding freeze-dried acai powder is even easier: scoop and dump. But you'll have to do just a bit more work to get the rest of your ingredients ready to blend.

WASH EVERYTHING

Because your produce is going from the ground, to a truck, to a processing plant, to a truck, and then to your grocery store before it gets to your kitchen, you'll want to make sure to clean it. But before you go scrubbing your entire grocery haul, think about what you're actually going to use in the next day or two. Washing fruit and veggies can lead to quicker spoilage, especially for delicate items like strawberries. Instead, you want to wash your produce just before you use it. If you know you'll be pressed for time in the morning, go ahead and get everything ready the night before. Just don't batch-prep a week's worth of smoothies on Sunday unless you want anything after Thursday to taste a little off.

The FDA recommends you start by washing your hands with warm water and soap for at least twenty seconds before you wash produce. You'll want to wash everything, even if you're going to peel it, to avoid cross contamination from the knife as you're peeling and slicing. For leafy greens or anything with nooks and crannies, let it soak in a water bath for two minutes before using your hands to gently remove any leftover dirt and debris. If you're prepping produce in advance, pat everything dry before storing it in the refrigerator. But if you're going to use your produce right away, don't worry about drying it—a little extra liquid in the blender won't hurt anything.

GET THINGS BLENDER-READY

Any of the produce that's going in your acai-powered smoothie or smoothie-bowl base will need to be prepped for the blender. Start by removing anything you wouldn't want to drink in a smoothie—stems, inedible peels, pits, and so on. It's especially important to remove apple seeds, which can be toxic if blended and ingested, and citrus membranes, which can make your smoothie taste bitter.

Next, slice everything up. Don't worry about chopping things finely or making it look pretty—it's going into a blender, which will do most of the work when you whip up your smoothie. (If you're going to be using any of your washed produce as smoothie-bowl toppings, you can be a little more meticulous with your slicing efforts.) And if you have a top-of-the-line blender, you might not have to do any chopping at all. Check the instruction manual that came with yours (or look it up online) to find out whether your ingredients need to be cut to a certain size for it to operate well.

FREEZE YOUR OWN FRUIT (AND VEGGIES)

Although you could use ice to create that cold, creamy smoothie consistency, using frozen fruit instead gives your drink a flavorful and nutritious boost. That means you'll always want some frozen fruit on hand—especially bananas, because they're an acai-smoothie staple that keeps your blends thick and creamy. (If you're not crazy about bananas, you can stock frozen avocados, mangoes, or peaches instead.)

You can find all kinds of frozen fruit in your supermarket's freezer aisle that is prepped and ready to blend into a delicious, healthful acai smoothie. But you can also easily freeze your own, which can be cheaper when fruit is in season or on sale. And you still get the benefits of ease and convenience when you make your morning smoothie while also avoiding any food waste.

If you want to freeze veggies, you'll have to blanch them before freezing them (which sounds more complicated than it is). All you have to do is submerge the vegetable (peel and all) in boiling water for about two minutes, then immediately move it to a bowl filled with ice water to stop the cooking process. Blanching is a crucial step for vegetables. Not only does it help them keep their color, texture, flavor, and nutrients intact, it also stops the enzymes that lead to spoilage.

For fruits, prep them the same way you would for the blender: wash and dry them, get rid of anything you don't want to drink, and give everything a rough chop. Then, make room in the freezer. You're going to spread your fruit and veggies out in a single layer on a baking sheet and slip the whole thing into the freezer, where it will sit for three hours or more. Once it's all frozen solid, add everything to a freezer-safe zip-top bag or airtight container, remove any excess air, label it with a date, and toss it back into the freezer. Your freshly frozen produce will keep for up to one year.

CHOOSING A BLENDER

The only way to maximize the benefits of acai is to blend your own acai-powered smoothies and smoothie bowls. You get to control every aspect of the blend, from the sugar to the flavors and the nutrients. And as soon as you get comfortable making your own smoothies (which won't be long!), you'll wonder how you ever lived without them.

You've probably noticed, though, that some things depend on the type of blender you choose. So how do you pick the right one? If you already own one you love, you're all set. But if you're in the market for one, keep reading for some tips on getting what you need for the best acai smoothies and bowls.

UNDERSTAND FUNCTIONALITY
A blender is one of those great go-to, multitasking appliances that have several functions. Depending on the model, you can make not only smoothies but also homemade soups, nut butters, hummus, sauces, salad dressings, and even ice cream. The sky (and your culinary skill) is the limit.

If you're looking to do more than make smoothies, you'll want some more impressive features. Look for higher-powered blenders with multiple speeds and a larger capacity. But if you're just starting out and want to make sure you like acai smoothies before you commit to something that serious, go for an inexpensive personal blender. You can always make up for motor power with some extra chopping.

THINK ABOUT VOLUME
When buying a blender, it's important to keep your lifestyle in mind. If you're just one person looking to whip up a quick morning acai smoothie, you might not need more than a personal bullet blender. These come with attachments that make it easy to blend and go. But if you have a family of five and don't feel like making everyone individual blends, then you'll need something that can handle a little more volume. Look for a traditional blender with a large pitcher.

STICK TO YOUR BUDGET
You can find blenders in pretty much every price range, from ten dollars to several hundred dollars. Therefore, it's important to know not only what features you're looking for in a blender, but also what price range you'd like to find them in. The 10-Day Acai-Powered Wellness Challenge is about making healthy choices work for you. If you're going to feel terrible about spending money on a high-priced blender, go for a less expensive option. But if you know you need the added incentive of a fancy blender or the guilt of an expensive one to drive you, go for it! Do what works for you. Just make sure you're comfortable with whatever price you pay.

CONSIDER THE CLEANUP

Love the idea of making healthful acai smoothies and bowls but hate the idea of yet another thing to clean? There's a blender for that. Some have fewer moving parts, some are dishwasher safe, and some even have a self-cleaning feature—just add some warm water and dish soap to the bowl, and watch it go! If you have a blender that fills you with dread for the cleanup that ensues every time you use it, you've got the wrong blender. It'll be worth replacing it with one that cleans easily if it means you'll use it more.

PICK ONE YOU LIKE

Again, this is about making your new routine work for you. That means picking a blender that takes your lifestyle and tastes into account. Do you love a clear countertop? Make sure your blender fits in a cupboard and that it's easy to lift (especially when you're tired and maybe don't feel like breaking out the blender). Or do you want a beautiful piece of machinery you can be proud to put on display? (In that case, make sure it's easy to clean. No one wants a dirty blender hanging out on the counter.)

If you're new to smoothie-making or you're just not a morning person, think about getting a blender with presets (buttons that tell you exactly what they do). Or even get one with fewer functions. If you love playing with new tech, go all out. You never know what that fancy new blender will inspire you to create.

But don't discount the way the blender looks. This isn't about vanity—this is about being happy to adopt a healthy new habit in your home. If a hot pink blender will make you smile, then that's the one you should get (as long as it checks all the other boxes, of course).

CONSIDER BULLET-STYLE BLENDERS

Bullet-style blenders are personal blenders that are shaped like bullets—a slim cup on top of a slim base. The blades screw right onto the cup, which you invert onto the base. Usually, you control bullet blenders by simply pressing down on the cup to pulse and twisting the cup to blend. But some do have buttons and multiple functions.

Bullet-style blenders will make one to two servings and take up the least amount of counter space, plus they often come with drinking lids that turn the blending cups into travel cups. (They also tend to come with multiple blending cups, which means you don't have to wash a cup every single day.) And both the cup and blades slip right into the top rack of the dishwasher. That makes bullet blenders the most convenient option for one person looking to add a healthy smoothie habit to their routine with the least amount of fuss. Although, with multiple cups, it also works for creating separate blends for multiple people.

Bullet-style blenders are the simplest option, but you can still find them in a variety of powers and prices. Look for one that's optimized for frozen fruit so that you have the option of making thicker smoothie-bowl bases in addition to drinkable smoothies.

CONSIDER HIGH-PERFORMANCE BLENDERS

As you can imagine, high-performance blenders are super-efficient at making superfood smoothies and bowls. They can handle anything you throw at them, from large chunks of fruit to whole nuts, and make quick work of it all. They'll also create an incredibly smooth consistency, regardless of ingredients.

These professional-style machines have the typical blender body—a pitcher with a blade in the bottom sitting on an electric base. They'll usually have multiple features, which means multiple buttons and presets. Some even have timers, self-cleaning functionality, and serving settings.

Size-wise, high-performance blenders tend to take up a fair amount of space. The base is larger to accommodate the blender's power, and the pitcher is larger to accommodate four or more smoothie servings. These are the multitasking machines you want if you're going to use your blender to make everything from soup to homemade nut butters.

A high-performance blender is a great option for someone who's committed to making healthy foods at home, someone whose whole family is in on the acai-smoothie-bowl fun, or someone who likes to make a few servings at a time. And you don't have to fret about your budget—you can find high-performance blenders at the same price as some of the better bullet-style blenders. Just make sure yours has enough blending power for all that you hope to do with it.

CONSIDER TRADITIONAL COUNTERTOP BLENDERS

Still not sure what to buy? A middle-of-the-road blender could be exactly what you need. Like the high-performance blenders, traditional machines look like what you picture when you think of a blender: glass or plastic pitcher on an electric base. They're often easy to maintain, with dishwasher-safe parts, and they can hold two to four servings. Traditional blenders are usually the least expensive of all the options, hovering somewhere around $20.

These blenders are a great option if you're still testing out your smoothie-making chops and getting familiar with a new routine. Because they're inexpensive, they may not hold up to rigorous use over time. But you can always upgrade to a better blender once you realize how delicious acai smoothies are and how great you feel when you have them. And you'll know exactly what you need in a new blender because you have hands-on experience.

USING A BLENDER

When you bring a new blender home, make sure you go through the box and familiarize yourself with all the pieces and features. Even the most tech-savvy among us needs to read the instructions. In fact, even if you have an old blender, dig out that instruction manual. Blenders are like people—they all have their quirks. The manufacturer knows what the blender likes, and you can save yourself a lot of time and trouble by reading about it rather than figuring it out yourself. Here are some other tips and how-to's to keep in mind when blending.

PREP YOUR PRODUCE

You already know the basics, like making sure to wash your produce not long before using it. But how to chop your fruits and veggies is going to depend on your particular blender. (This is why it comes in handy to read the manual.) For example, some blenders require you to cut up your ingredients rather well, while others can take anything you throw at them. Most fall somewhere in between. The best way to know what yours prefers is to read the instructions.

However you're required to chop your produce, you'll want to remove any seeds, stems, pits, and inedible peels. This isn't because your blender can't handle them—some can. It's because you don't want to have to strain your blend. One of the best things about acai smoothies is their nutrient profiles. You're packing a lot of vitamins, minerals, and antioxidants into a single glass. But straining your blend can remove some of those nutrients, as can peeling your fruit. A lot of the nutrients found in fruits and veggies come from their skins. If you want the most nutrient-rich smoothie or bowl, skip the peeling process with apples, berries, pears, peaches, plums, carrots, and cucumbers. You'll have to test your blender, but you shouldn't even notice a difference in texture.

KEEP YOUR DISTANCE

This should go without saying, but *do not* ever put your hands into the blender or near the blade when the blender is plugged in. It doesn't matter whether it's on—you could accidentally lean on a button. This is a "better safe than sorry" situation. A few quick pulses should move your ingredients into position with no problem, but you can also use the tamper that came with your blender or a wooden spoon to push the produce toward the blades.

USE FROZEN FRUITS

Some recipes use ice to create the traditional consistency of a smoothie, but the better way to do it is to use frozen fruit, which gives you an even smoother texture, better flavor, and more nutrients. Bananas, avocados, peaches, and mangoes are the best fruits to use for your base.

You can regulate the thickness of your smoothie with your frozen-to-fresh-fruit ratio. The more frozen fruits you add, the thicker your smoothie. The more fresh fruits you add, the thinner your smoothie. Although fruits aren't the only thickener you'll use, they are the foundation for your acai-powered smoothie. When you get into smoothie bowls, you'll use more frozen fruit to create a thicker base for toppings.

ADD ANOTHER THICKENER

Often, you'll add another yummy thickening ingredient like yogurt or nut butter to your smoothie. This is especially the case if you're using more fresh than frozen fruit. Not only will thickeners up the creaminess quotient of your smoothie, they'll also add to the flavor profile. Think: raspberry yogurt in an acai-peach smoothie, or peanut butter in an acai-strawberry bowl. The flavor of your thickener can have a big impact.

Thickeners usually have the added benefit of protein, making a smoothie more filling and energizing. Just consider the overall sugar content of your smoothie when deciding on your thickener. If it feels a little high in added sugar, choose an unsweetened option.

TOP IT WITH LIQUID

Although you don't want to water down your smoothie, you'll need to add some sort of liquid to help the blender do its job—it ensures that the blade runs smoothly and that the ingredients bind together. You can use any sort of liquid you like to get the flavor profile and consistency you want. Trying for a tropical smoothie? Add coconut water to your blend. Hoping for something that tastes like a PB&J milkshake? Use cashew or almond milk. You could also use regular milk, soymilk, coconut milk, juice, or even plain old water. Whichever you choose, stick to the unsweetened options so that your acai smoothie doesn't become a sugar bomb. And start with just ¼ cup per serving, increasing the amount until you get the desired consistency.

BLEND IN STAGES

A high-speed, high-performance blender should have no problem with your throwing all the ingredients in at once. But for smaller, traditional, and personal blenders, you may want to work in stages to avoid any unblended chunks of fruit sticking to your straw. Start with any leafy greens or nuts, and pre-blend them before adding the other ingredients. Next, add the acai puree and frozen fruits. If you have a lot of frozen fruits, blend them in a few at a time. Then blend in the fresh fruits, followed by the thickener. Last but not least, pour in the liquid a little at a time until you reach the consistency you want. If your blender is still having a bit of trouble, just keep blending. The heat from the blades will help break down your frozen fruit and, eventually, make everything nice and creamy.

ENJOYING YOUR SMOOTHIE

Recipes aren't written in stone. And one of the great things about both the 10-Day Acai-Powered Wellness Challenge and acai smoothies in general is that you get to make the healthy habits work for you. Add the ingredients you like, swap out the ones you don't, and never drink something that doesn't taste good to you. In other words, do what you need to do to create acai-powered smoothies and bowls you love. This is all about making your new wellness routine work for you. And the best way to do that is to make sure you enjoy every nutritious sip and spoonful!

TRY IT OUT

Before you pour your finished smoothie into a glass, grab a spoon and taste a little bit of it. You can always add a couple of ingredients to get the flavor just right. If your blend is a little bitter, add more sweet fruit or a drizzle of honey. If it's too sweet, add more acai or nut butter. And if you discover that a blend is beyond repair, throw it out and start fresh!

MAKE IT YOUR OWN

When you're just starting out, it's best to give a recipe the benefit of the doubt. Maybe you're not crazy about spinach, but nine times out of ten, you won't even know it's in your smoothie. But if there's ever an ingredient that you know you hate, or if there's something you're allergic to, don't hesitate to make a swap. Just try to substitute like for like. For example, you can switch out a green for another green, or a sweet fruit for another sweet fruit. You'll find bananas in almost every smoothie recipe because they make a great base. If you're not a fan, just swap them out for another thickener like avocado or mango.

DRINK IT FRESH

Just like the produce in your grocery store, the produce in your acai-powered smoothie starts losing nutrients the minute you make it. Drink your blends as soon as possible. If you can't drink one right away, store it in an airtight container in the refrigerator for up to 24 hours, or freeze it in an airtight container until you're ready for it. And whenever you store your smoothie for later, make sure you shake or stir it before you drink it. (Some of the ingredients may separate and sink to the bottom when they're left sitting.)

MAKING AMAZING SMOOTHIE BOWLS

One of the many miracles of acai is that it creates such an amazing foundation for other healthful and delicious ingredients—and not all the ingredients need to go in the blender. That means that you get to include beneficial foods that taste wonderful together even when they don't physically blend well.

Another benefit of smoothie bowls is that they are scientifically proven to feel more satisfying than smoothies because you eat them with a spoon. (The physical act of chewing makes a big difference to your brain.) So now it's time to add the flavor and crunch you've been craving by learning how to turn any acai-powered smoothie into a deliciously filling and nutritious acai-powered smoothie bowl.

CREATE YOUR SMOOTHIE-BOWL BASE

You can find an endless variety of acai-powered smoothie-bowl recipes for every palate and health concern (including a bunch toward the back of this very book). But it can be very helpful to know how to turn a regular acai smoothie recipe into a smoothie-bowl base, or even how to create a base from scratch. Then, whenever you're in the mood for a superpowered snack, you can just whip one up.

The most important thing to keep in mind is that your smoothie-bowl base should be thick enough to support toppings. To turn a drinkable smoothie recipe into a smoothie-bowl base, you'll want to use less liquid and more thickening ingredients. That could mean using frozen fruit instead of fresh; adding creamier fruits like banana, avocado, or mango to the mix; or blending in additional yogurt or nut butter.

To create a smoothie-bowl base from scratch, you can follow a simple formula: 1 packet of frozen acai puree, 1 frozen banana, 1 cup frozen fruit, 1 tablespoon nut butter, and ½ cup liquid. This will make one large serving or two small servings of thick smoothie-bowl base. (And obviously, you can play with the ratios once you learn what you like in a smoothie bowl.)

KEEP IT COLORFUL

Just seeing pictures of beautiful acai bowls on social media can make you crave one. When done right, they're lovely works of edible art. Slices of fresh fruit, drizzles of nut butters and honey, and sprinklings of toasted coconut flakes and even dark chocolate make your mouth water. That's the kind of bowl you want to create, because it will make you *want* to eat healthy. But it can take a bit of practice to make these picture-perfect bowls.

For one thing, consider that your acai puree is already a deep, dark color. Now try to remember what happened in art class when you were little and mixed a bunch of paint colors together. (You got brown.) If you want a bright, picture-worthy bowl that whets your appetite, avoid throwing every kind of ingredient into the blender at first. Start out with an acai blend of frozen strawberries, raspberries, and blueberries for a vivid berry-colored bowl. When you realize how delicious *all* acai bowls are, and that you can cover any blend with a beautiful variety of toppings, you'll care less about the color of the base.

ADD BITE-SIZE TOPPINGS

Aesthetics are important, but so is practicality. It's easier to eat a bowl with bite-size slices of fruit than one thoughtfully garnished with whole strawberries. The same goes for whole figs, pineapple rounds, and any other bright, beautiful topping you're tempted to leave on the larger side for the sake of a pretty bowl. You have to eat your acai bowl with a spoon, often when you're already pressed for time. Don't make more work for yourself. Dice everything up so that it easily fits on a spoon, ensuring that every single bite is packed with tasty nutrition.

MAKE IT PHOTO-WORTHY

Dicing your fruit doesn't mean giving up on your acai masterpiece. In fact, bite-size fruit can make your bowl more appealing with the ultimate acai-bowl trick: rows. Browse through posts of acai bowls, and you're bound to notice neat lines of toppings in nearly every photo.

Acai bowls may taste like ice cream sundaes sometimes, but you don't want to dump the toppings into the bowl like a kid at the self-serve frozen-yogurt station. Messy bowls aren't appetizing. But neat rows of crunchy seeds, white coconut, and brightly colored fresh fruit are. Finish things off with an artful drizzle of nut butter or honey for the ultimate visual impact and flavor profile.

And when you create a particularly beautiful bowl, go ahead and share it on social media. Sharing your wellness journey with friends can help hold you accountable and make you more likely to stick with healthy new habits. And who knows—you might inspire others to embrace the acai miracle!

EXPERIMENT WITH FLAVOR
You may be realizing that making a smoothie bowl is an art, not a science—so get creative! You can replicate almost any flavor in healthy smoothie-bowl form, like chocolate peanut-butter pretzel and orange creamsicle. And the available toppings stretch as far as your imagination. Just make sure the flavors complement each other in both the base and the toppings. And remember the golden rule: less is more.

KEEP THINGS SIMPLE
You might be tempted to cover every inch of your acai bowl in toppings, but that's a quick way to overwhelm your taste buds. You'll get tired of your bowl halfway through, and that defeats the whole purpose of adding yummy toppings. You want every addition to enhance the flavor and nutrient profile of your bowl, which means being selective.

When you use just a few flavors that complement each other, each of the ingredients really shines. Create four thin rows of toppings at the most and leave about a quarter of your smoothie surface showing. That ensures not only a picture-perfect bowl, but also one you'll want to finish.

SKIP THE ADDED SUGARS
From the acai to your liquid and your thickeners, there are plenty of places for added sugar to hide in a smoothie. Just imagine how much sugar you can add to a smoothie bowl through toppings! That's why some nutritionists describe acai bowls as "sugar bombs," meant to be used as an occasional treat—one bowl can contain twice the maximum recommended amount of sugar. But that doesn't have to be the case if you're thoughtful about your bowl's ingredients.

Creating delicious acai bowls is about giving your body the nutrition it needs to thrive, but you still need to make wellness work for you. So there's no shame in wanting a little something sweet in your bowl. Just be mindful when adding sweetened ingredients, choosing just one or two small ways to introduce sweetness, like a drizzle of honey or sweetened coconut flakes.

And during the 10-Day Acai-Powered Wellness Challenge, try to go cold-turkey on added sugar. After just a few days, you'll notice that your body no longer craves it. Plus, you'll really start to taste the natural sweetness of your acai bowl's ingredients—especially the fruit. (They don't call fruit "nature's candy" for nothing!)

EAT IT SKILLFULLY

Believe it or not, there are even a few tips for how to eat your acai bowl. Although you'll want to savor each amazing bite of your acai-powered smoothie bowl, you'll need to do it quickly. Like other frozen treats, smoothie bowls are best enjoyed quickly. (Unless you're a fan of "ice cream soup"—then go ahead and let your bowl melt.)

And if you're a stickler for proportionate bites, you'll want to eat your bowl from the bottom up. (This is where it comes in handy to leave a quarter of the bowl uncovered.) That way, you don't run out of scrumptious toppings before you've finished your smoothie base.

ENJOY YOUR MASTERPIECE!

It may take a few tries to create the kind of bowl that makes you say "Wow," but you're on your way to beautiful smoothie bowls. You never know— you might knock it out of the park on your first try. Just don't give up if your first few attempts go awry. Every not-so-great bowl will help you figure out how to create the kind of bowl you love to eat, which will bring you closer to the happier, healthier you that you're working toward. So savor every nutritious spoonful of acai-powered smoothie bowl, and celebrate every artful creation. Not only are you gaining a new skill, you're also creating the life you want to live. And that's pretty amazing!

Powerful Partners

You know how miraculous acai is. And you know that its superpower is acting as the foundation for superfood smoothies and smoothie bowls. But now you need to know how to create the most impactful blends for your wellness journey.

Understanding what each fruit, vegetable, seed, grain, and nut brings to the nutritional table is key to creating a healthy habit that helps you reach your goals. Because you're not like everyone else. A one-size-fits-all approach won't work for you. You need a flexible plan that gives you the information you need to tailor acai-powered wellness to your body.

This section covers the most popular and powerful options that you can add to your acai blends and bowls. You'll learn what they have to offer and how to use them. Just make sure you change things up every so often so that you get the full slate of nutrients available. And as you read on, feel free to daydream about the incredible blends you're going to create!

FRUITS AND VEGGIES

Fruit is the foundation of any smoothie or smoothie bowl, so it's even more important to make sure that you choose fruits with the best health benefits. And you might not realize that you can sneak a fair number of veggies into your blend without it tasting like a wheatgrass-filled green juice. Check out these smoothie-blend staples for inspiration.

APPLES

Antioxidant-rich apples help protect your heart health, bone health, and brain function while also lowering your risk of stroke, easing digestion, boosting immunity, balancing blood sugar, and reducing harmful inflammation, thanks to their prebiotic properties, flavonols, and polyphenols. Just remember to remove their toxic seeds before adding apples to your blend or bowl.

AVOCADOS

With healthy doses of monounsaturated fat, carotenoids, potassium, and fiber, avocados can help lower your blood pressure and cholesterol, protect your eye health, ease your digestion, and help you maintain a healthy weight. Plus, they make your smoothie blends extra creamy, even acting as a substitute for the ever-present smoothie staple, banana.

BEETS

Beets are well known for protecting your heart and brain function by boosting blood flow. They can also help reduce inflammation, improve kidney function, and support healthy digestion. Adding beets to your blend is a great way to give it a bright red hue, but keep in mind that, like acai, their flavor is on the earthy side. Make sure you add something sweet to balance things out.

BLACKBERRIES

In addition to being delicious as both blend ingredient and bowl topping, blackberries are chock-full of vitamins, minerals, and fiber. They're especially high in immune-boosting vitamin C and blood-clotting vitamin K. And, like most berries, they help fend off free radicals and protect your brain with a bevy of antioxidants. Because they're similar in flavor to acai, you might want to add a sweet ingredient or two to your blackberry-acai blends.

BLUEBERRIES

Adding blueberries to your acai blends is a no-brainer—they go together like peanut butter and jelly! But blueberries also offer a huge antioxidant boost that can help lower your blood pressure, prevent heart disease, improve brain function, and reduce insulin sensitivity in people with type 2 diabetes. Double up on this superfood by using it both in your base and as a topping.

CHERRIES

Although cherries are technically drupes, and therefore not related to berries, they still pack that berry-like antioxidant punch, which makes them powerful anti-inflammatories. Cherries have also been shown to boost recovery after exercise and benefit heart health with their potassium and polyphenols. Tart cherries can be blended in but also make a great topping, especially when paired with heart-healthy dark chocolate shavings.

COCONUT

Like other fruits, coconut contains its fair share of antioxidants. But it also contains protein, fiber, and several important minerals, like manganese, copper, and iron. With that nutritional profile, coconut can help protect your heart, balance your blood sugar, fight inflammation, and keep your bones healthy. You can add coconut to your blends by mixing in coconut water or milk or topping your bowl with coconut flakes, which can be raw, toasted, sweetened, or unsweetened.

CRANBERRIES

Adding cranberries to a blend can give it a delightfully fall flavor while bringing all the benefits of antioxidants and polyphenols. Although the jury is still out on whether cranberries actually help with UTIs, they can definitely help protect your heart, reduce inflammation, and boost your brain function. Whether you use fresh or dried cranberries in your blend or bowl, balance cranberry's tart flavor with creamy ingredients like almond milk.

CUCUMBERS

When you're in the mood for a super-hydrating smoothie, cucumbers are a great addition. They're chock-full of antioxidants, plus their pectin and high water content support healthy digestion, weight loss, and balanced blood sugar. Don't bother peeling them—they keep a ton of nutrients in their skins.

FIGS

Figs not only take a picture-perfect smoothie bowl to a whole new level, they also pack in the fiber, calcium, antioxidants, and a bunch of other vitamins and minerals. In fact, they're one of the richest plant sources of several vitamins and minerals. That makes figs great for balancing your blood sugar, clearing your skin, strengthening hair, and fending off free radicals.

GOJI BERRIES

Goji berries are good for your eyes, skin, immune system, blood sugar, and even your feeling of well-being. You'll often see dried goji berries scattered over beautiful acai bowls, but they can also be blended right into the smoothie base. (Look for them in small bags in the health food aisle of your grocery store.)

KALE

With an almost absurd amount of vitamins, minerals, and antioxidants, superfood kale helps prevent the oxidative stress that can lead to chronic illness and cancer, gives you more energy, reduces your risk of diabetes, protects your heart, and even helps your blood clot. Just make sure you counterbalance kale's bitterness with other sweet ingredients.

KIWI

If you're looking to shore up your acai blends with even more superfoods, adding kiwis is a must. Studies show kiwi can aid digestion, boost immune health, fight inflammation, help manage blood pressure, reduce blood clotting, protect against vision loss, and even help treat asthma. Not to mention it's delicious as both a blend ingredient and a beautiful bowl topping.

LEMONS AND LIMES

Lemon and lime are bright additions to any blend, but especially a tropical smoothie. They also pack in the immune-boosting benefits of vitamin C and the free-radical fighting benefits of other antioxidants. Plus, their citric acid can help prevent the formation of kidney stones. Citrus membranes can make a smoothie taste bitter, so just squeeze lemon or lime juice straight into your blend rather than adding the whole fruit.

MANGO

Mangoes are full of vitamin C, fiber, and beta-carotene, making them great additions to any recipe that hopes to boost immune health, protect eyes, or improve digestion. Blend frozen mango into your smoothie-bowl base to thicken it, or dice it up for a tropical topping. (Preferably both!)

ORANGES

Although oranges are well known for their immune-boosting vitamin C, they can also help prevent heart disease thanks to their potassium, the flavonoid hesperidin, and a good amount of fiber. Oranges should be either carefully sectioned to remove the membranes or, like lemons and limes, they can just contribute juice to your blend to avoid any bitterness.

PEACHES

Like many fruits, peaches are full of fiber and antioxidants, so they can aid digestion and fight inflammation. But unlike other fruits, they can also improve your skin and reduce allergy symptoms. You can use peaches both in your blends and as a topping. They're also another great alternative to bananas for use as a thickener when frozen.

POMEGRANATE SEEDS

Pomegranate seeds are another smart addition to an acai-powered superfood smoothie. And because they're as pretty as jewels, they make an especially lovely addition to smoothie bowls. These little seeds pack in large amounts of fiber, protein, vitamins C and K, folate, and potassium. In addition to fighting inflammation, boosting brain function, and lowering the risk for heart disease, pomegranate seeds may also help fight prostate and breast cancers.

PINEAPPLE

Nothing brightens up acai quite like pineapple, especially in a bowl topped with coconut, mango, and more pineapple! This amazing fruit is so full of vitamin C and other antioxidants that it beats oranges for immune-boosting properties. It's also a great addition to digestive blends because it contains bromelain, a group of digestive enzymes that can help your body break down food.

PUMPKIN
You might not think that acai and pumpkin blend well, but they're perfect complements for a bowl that's not too sweet. You can even find recipes for blends that taste like pumpkin pie! And this winter squash offers more than flavor—it's also packed with antioxidants. It's also very low in calories for its nutritional content, which makes it a smart choice when you're trying to maintain a healthy weight.

ROMAINE LETTUCE
If dark, leafy greens aren't your thing, consider adding romaine to your blends instead. It not only is refreshing and hydrating, but also contains free-radical-fighting antioxidants, immune-boosting vitamin C, heart-healthy folate and potassium, and vision-loving vitamin A. Toss a small handful into your blender before adding the frozen fruit.

SPINACH
Some acai enthusiasts add spinach to every blend and bowl because of its powerful health benefits (and the fact that you can't even taste it). Spinach can protect your body, heart, and brain against oxidative stress while boosting your immune system, nourishing your eyes, and contributing to strong bones. Why wouldn't you want to add all that to your smoothie?

STRAWBERRIES
Adding the bright, sweet-tart flavor of strawberries to your acai bowl base and toppings is a no-brainer. But you'll also be adding antioxidants, vitamins, minerals, and phytochemicals that can help lower your risk of heart disease, fight oxidative stress, reduce inflammation, lower your cholesterol, regulate your blood sugar, and prevent certain types of cancer. Not bad for something that delicious!

UBE
Ube's sweet, nutty flavor and bright purple color are perfect complements for acai. If you're in the United States, you may not have heard of this purple yam, but ube is a staple in its native home of the Philippines for a reason. It's a great source of potassium, vitamin C, and antioxidants. Two of the anthocyanins in purple yams—cyanidin and peonidin—have even been shown to fight colon, lung, and prostate cancers.

YOGURTS
Although you don't want to go overboard on the dairy, it still offers plenty of benefits—including calcium and probiotics—in moderation and in the right forms.

GREEK-STYLE YOGURT
With all of yogurt's calcium, vitamins, minerals, and probiotics, it's a smart choice for any smoothie and bowl that's focused on building strong bones, easing digestion, or maintaining a healthy weight. It's also handy for thickening your blend. Although flavored yogurts can add some punch to smoothies and bowls, try to stick to unsweetened Greek-style yogurts for the most nutritional benefit.

KEFIR
If you're not familiar with kefir, it is a fermented beverage made with cow's milk or goat's milk, and it's becoming increasingly popular among smoothie enthusiasts for its many nutritional benefits (and the fact that it helps thicken things up). It has more powerful probiotics than yogurt, it has antibacterial properties, and it can strengthen bones, aid digestion, and improve allergy and asthma symptoms. Kefir is also low in lactose.

NUTS, NUT MILKS, AND NUT BUTTERS
Nuts are a common addition to acai smoothies and bowls because they're so versatile. In addition to using chopped nuts as a bowl topping, you can use almond and cashew nut butters and milks. And while walnuts are the third most popular choice, not many people would turn down a topping of chocolate-hazelnut spread. No matter what form you find them in, nuts are both delicious and nutritious additions to your blends. Just stick to the unsweetened varieties whenever possible to keep your smoothies focused on wellness.

ALMONDS
Just a small handful of almonds provides plenty of fiber, protein, and fatty acids, not to mention 37 percent of your recommended daily amount of vitamin E. Vitamin E is an antioxidant that can boost your immune health and protect your heart while fighting off the oxidative stress that leads to chronic illness and even cancer. Almonds are also a great choice if you're watching your weight or your blood sugar. Whether you chop whole almonds for a topping, add a dollop of almond butter to your blend, or use almond milk as your liquid, you can't go wrong with almonds.

CASHEWS

The buttery taste of heart-healthy cashews makes them a scrumptious addition to your smoothies and bowls in the form of cashew butter and cashew milk, but using them as a topper, too, doesn't hurt. In fact, the more cashews the better, since they're packed with vitamins, minerals, and antioxidants. In addition to the benefits of antioxidants, the copper and iron in cashews help the body form and use red blood cells, which support your blood vessels, bones, nerves, and immune system. Plus, the lutein and zeaxanthin protect your eye health.

WALNUTS

Walnuts are more than just a delicious topping for acai bowls—they're also an absolute powerhouse of nutrition. They have higher antioxidant activity than any other nut thanks to their vitamin E, melatonin, and polyphenols. Plus they're packed with omega-3 fatty acids. All that means that walnuts are great for your heart, brain, immune system, blood sugar, digestion, and weight. And they fight the inflammation that can lead to diseases like Alzheimer's and cancer. Not bad for a little nut!

SEEDS

Acai smoothies and bowls are a great way to reap the health benefits of ingredients you wouldn't ordinarily incorporate into your diet. Each of the seeds described here packs a huge nutritional punch and adds some crunchy flavor to your smoothie blends.

CHIA SEEDS

Chia seeds are tiny but mighty, packing in fiber, protein, vitamins, minerals, antioxidants, and omega-3 fatty acids (even more than salmon). These little guys can fight inflammation, protect your heart, reduce your blood sugar, help you maintain a healthy weight, and much more. They are always a worthy addition to an acai smoothie or bowl. When adding chia seeds to smoothies, soak them in a bit of water for a few minutes before adding them to your blend. Also give them a few minutes as a bowl topping to allow them to gel up before you dig in.

FLAX SEEDS

Flax seeds are full of heart-healthy fiber and omega-3 fatty acids, not to mention high-quality protein that can help you maintain a healthy weight. Although many people top their acai bowls with flax seeds, others think they have a better texture when blended directly into the smoothie itself. Try it both ways and see what you like!

HEMP SEEDS

The protein, vitamins, minerals, and fatty acids in hemp seeds (also known as hemp hearts) can help reduce your risk of heart disease, improve skin disorders, aid digestion, and even reduce symptoms of PMS and menopause. Plus, their nutty flavor makes them a tasty topping for acai smoothie bowls.

PUMPKIN SEEDS

You might think of pumpkin seeds as the things you dig out of a pumpkin and roast, but in this context, pumpkin seeds (or *pepitas*) are the shelled, green insides of those seeds that you can find at the supermarket. These easy-to-eat seeds are rich in antioxidants, magnesium, and fiber and make a yummy topping for acai bowls. They'll help you balance your blood sugar, improve your sleep, protect your heart, and strengthen your bones.

OTHER PLANT PRODUCTS

Although a fruit smoothie seems very different from a green juice, they have a lot in common. Smoothies rely more heavily on fruit, but that doesn't mean you can't use a few of the tricks of green drinks. Herbs, roots, spices, and even wheatgrass can make a tasty and powerful addition to acai smoothie blends.

GINGER

When your stomach is upset, adding ginger to your smoothie blend is a no-brainer. But this little root can do more than ease digestion and soothe stomachs. It can also ease arthritis pain, lower blood sugar and cholesterol, protect against heart disease, and inhibit bacterial growth. To add it to a stomach-soothing acai smoothie, use about ½ teaspoon of grated ginger per serving.

MINT

If you're not sure how you feel about mint in your acai blend, just remember how good mojitos and mint-chocolate-chip ice cream are. You can recreate both in a healthful smoothie or bowl. The smell of mint alone can boost brain function, but it also contains neuroprotective antioxidants. Plus, it can help relieve digestive troubles.

TURMERIC

Another superfood that took the nation by storm, this brightly colored spice not only has antioxidant effects itself but also increases the body's capacity for antioxidants from other sources. So turmeric gives twice the anti-inflammatory, brain-boosting, and heart-protecting benefits. Turmeric has also been shown both to fight certain cancers and to treat them, as well as help ward off chronic and degenerative illnesses. A little goes a long way, so just add about ½ teaspoon of turmeric for every serving of smoothie.

WHEATGRASS
Wheatgrass is a staple of green drinks and juice bars everywhere for good reason. It tastes like green tea and contains vitamins and antioxidants that can help lower cholesterol, regulate blood sugar, reduce inflammation, and support weight loss. Just make sure you pre-blend wheatgrass before adding frozen fruit, to avoid any texture issues.

CEREALS AND WHOLE GRAINS
Whether you need a little crunch for the top of your acai bowl or a little extra thickness in your smoothie, these humble ingredients offer that and more. They're filled with vitamins, minerals, antioxidants, and healthy fats.

GRANOLA
Granola is a crunchy mixture of many things, usually including oats, flax seeds, chia seeds, and almonds. That means that granola contains all their benefits, too, including antioxidants, fiber, and fatty acids. Just keep in mind that granola can be a calorie and sugar bomb if you don't choose carefully. Look for low-fat, low-sugar varieties with only ingredients you can pronounce.

OATMEAL
Not only is oatmeal filling, which means it can help you maintain a healthy weight, it can also help protect your heart, ease digestion, and lower blood sugar and cholesterol levels. Like yogurt and nut butters, oatmeal makes a great thickening agent in acai smoothies and bowls. Just make sure you pre-blend it to grind it up before adding the other smoothie ingredients.

PUFFED RICE
As a topping, puffed rice contributes a delectable light crunch to your acai bowls while also adding vitamins, minerals, fiber, protein, and energy-boosting carbs. It can aid digestion, strengthen bones, boost your immune system and brain function, and help you feel more satisfied after eating.

Put Acai to Good Use

Now that you have an idea of just how powerful acai smoothies and bowls are, are you ready to create an acai-powered habit that will last you the rest of your long, healthy life? Ready for more energy, better digestion, deeper sleep, improved mood, and a brain and body that fire on all cylinders? It's all just 10 days away! And you'll get to enjoy delicious acai smoothies and bowls along the way. You'll also enjoy movement that makes you happy and the downtime you need to unwind in the fully flexible 10-Day Acai-Powered Wellness Challenge. If you're ready to look and feel great, just turn the page!

PART 3

The 10-Day Acai-Powered Wellness Challenge

Are you ready to feel better than you ever have? Just ten days from now, you could have clearer skin, improved digestion, better brain function, a healthier heart, and a trimmer waistline! The 10-Day Acai-Powered Wellness Challenge makes it easy to transform your health with mouthwatering acai-centered recipes and a simple plan you'll actually *want* to follow.

This isn't a diet or a detox—this is a whole-health revolution. For ten days, you're going to put yourself first, giving your body the balance it craves while treating your taste buds to twice-daily superfood smoothies. And by the end of the challenge, you'll feel amazing!

And these ten days are just the jumping-off point for a long, happy, healthy life. The 10-Day Acai-Powered Wellness Challenge gives you the flexible framework you need to create healthy habits that stick. You'll learn how to harness the power of acai by combining it with nourishing meals, regular exercise, plenty of rest, and a positive mindset.

Once you're familiar with the plan, read on to discover how to make the most of those first ten days and really set yourself up for success. Then dive into Day 1 of the rest of your acai-powered life!

Your 10-Day Plan

The 10-Day Acai-Powered Wellness Challenge isn't some impossible task meant to torture you. It's a simple plan designed to help you succeed in setting up healthy habits that will last you a lifetime. And because a plan only works if you follow through on it, this one is completely customizable. You'll use the framework provided to ensure you're working *with* your body and not against it. But what you eat, when you eat, and how you move is entirely up to you. By Day 10, you'll feel so great you'll want to keep going!

FUEL YOUR HEALTH

Completing this challenge is a way to empower yourself and take back control of your health. And it's easier than you think—a few simple shifts are all you need. Instead of letting convenience dictate your day, you'll mindfully choose food and movement that fuel you. For best results, every day of your wellness challenge should include:

- **Homemade acai smoothies.** Each day, you'll whip up one recipe that you'll use for both a breakfast smoothie bowl and an afternoon smoothie snack. The recommended blends, which are chock-full of superfoods, are all designed to sustain you throughout your day with vitamins, minerals, antioxidants, and scrumptious flavors.
- **Protein-rich snacks.** Smoothie bowls can be a great source of protein if they include things like whole grains, nuts, seeds, and fortified milk (or nondairy-milk) products, but they alone can't give your body *everything* it needs to function well. Incorporating protein-rich snacks into your plan helps you stay full and energized while your body does the hard work of restoring itself.
- **Complete and balanced meals.** For the most health benefits, you'll need to balance acai-centered smoothies with nourishing meals. These should incorporate a variety of healthy proteins, fats, and carbohydrates, not to mention even more fruits and veggies (which should take up half your plate). Each day of the Wellness Challenge includes inspiration for your morning snack, lunch, and dinner, but feel free to eat whatever you like—as long as it's healthy and balanced!
- **Eight glasses of water.** Every one of your body's processes runs on water, including digesting your smoothie bowls and absorbing their nutrients. Although smoothies are hydrating, you'll still need to drink at least eight glasses of water each day to maximize the challenge's health benefits.
- **Regular exercise.** Although healthy eating has an incredible impact on your well-being, it can't replace the benefits of exercise—they go hand in hand to optimize your health. Moving your body for 30 minutes every day helps the acai work its magic. Choose a type of exercise that you enjoy so that those 30 minutes don't become a chore. Anything, from a long walk to a wild Zumba class, will do.
- **Mindfulness.** Real wellness is about more than just good physical health—it's also about good mental health. Practicing mindfulness has actually been shown to enhance both. It can help relieve anxiety and stress, lower your blood pressure, reduce chronic pain, and improve your sleep. Whether you choose to meditate, enjoy nature, or keep a gratitude journal, make mindfulness a part of each day.

FOCUS ON FEELING GOOD

While you're upping your intake of all things wholesome and healthy, you'll also want to steer clear of the habits that hold you back from wellness. (A nightly bowl of ice cream might make you feel good in the moment, but no one likes the sugar crash, weight gain, or cavities that follow.) Plus, by focusing on the things that make you feel good, you could find yourself craving the other stuff less and less. For these ten days, try to eliminate:

- **Alcohol.** The jury is still out on the potential health benefits of alcohol, but the dehydration, fermentation, and sleep disruption definitely aren't going to help you during your wellness challenge. Try to avoid alcohol entirely and see how you feel. After the challenge, you're welcome to work back in your nightly glass of red wine (and its antioxidants).
- **Negativity.** Worry and frustration can do more than affect your follow-through—they can also upset your health, causing problems like anxiety and high blood pressure. Practicing mindfulness during your challenge should help, but you'll want to catch yourself when you're headed down an unhelpful rabbit hole. Try to let go of the things you can't control and focus on the things you can—like your awesome new eating habits.
- **Processed foods.** You'll often know processed foods by the box, can, or bag with the long list of unpronounceable ingredients on the back. Don't be lulled by "low fat" labels, either. These can be some of the worst offenders, with chemical ingredients added to make up for the loss of flavor and texture. During your challenge, try to skip these items and instead shop the edges of the supermarket, where all the whole, healthful foods are.
- **Red meat.** This challenge is all about optimizing your health, which means staying away from anything that could put a strain on your heart. And since red meat has been linked to high cholesterol, high blood pressure, and heart disease, it certainly qualifies. If you can cut back and replace a few hamburgers with baked salmon, your heart will thank you for it. But to feel your very best, vegetarian options are the way to go.
- **Refined carbohydrates.** One of the easiest ways to meet your health goals is to eliminate refined carbs (think: sugary snacks, white bread, and pasta). Not only are these items usually devoid of nutrients, they can also clog your pores, make you gain weight, and contribute to conditions like type 2 diabetes and heart disease. But the good news is that the more refined carbs you cut, the fewer you crave.
- **Salt.** Excess sodium is linked to all sorts of health problems, from high blood pressure to stomach cancer. Whenever possible, choose low- or no-sodium alternatives to salty meals and snacks. Adding herbs or a splash of citrus can sometimes be all you need to up the flavor ante in a recipe.
- **Soda and seltzer.** Skipping sugary drinks during a wellness challenge is a no-brainer, but it's not just the sugar you need to worry about. Carbonation can also make you feel bloated and sluggish and, well, unwell. So skip the flavored seltzer water, too. If you're craving something sweet, reach for a small cup of freshly squeezed, sugar-free juice.

The 10-Day Acai-Powered Wellness Challenge

This is it! This is your time to shine. Give this challenge just ten days of your time and attention, and get ready to feel better than you have in years. As a reward for making it to the end of the challenge, you'll find that the recommended recipes get a bit sweeter as you go along. (Not into the sweet stuff? Go ahead and substitute those recipes for any of the other ones in the challenge.)

Each recipe creates two servings: one to use as your morning smoothie-bowl base and one to drink as your afternoon snack. If the base is a little too thick for your taste, just stir in a bit of liquid to dilute it. You could simply use water, or you could add a flavor boost with some nondairy milk or unsweetened juice. Remember, this challenge is all about creating healthy habits you can live with for the long run. Don't be afraid to tweak the snacks, meals, and smoothies to suit you!

DAY 1

Breakfast
Eat a challenge-approved smoothie bowl.

AM Snack
Eat a healthy snack.
Example: Kale chips.

Lunch
Eat a healthy lunch of your choice.
Example: Low-sodium minestrone soup.

PM Snack
Drink one 8- to 12-ounce challenge-approved acai smoothie.

Dinner
Eat a healthy meal of your choice.
Example: Marinated and grilled chicken-and-veggie kababs.

Daily Habits
- Drink at least 8 glasses of water.
- Get at least 30 minutes of exercise.
- Practice mindfulness (like gratitude or meditation) once a day.

Today's Recommended Wellness-Challenge Recipe

Fresh Start Smoothie
Servings: 2

Base and Smoothie
1 packet frozen acai puree (unsweetened)
1 medium frozen banana
½ cup frozen mixed berries
½ cup fresh mixed berries
½ cup almond milk
¼–½ cup preferred liquid to dilute (optional)

Suggested Bowl Toppings
Banana slices
Chia seeds
Low-fat granola
Toasted coconut chips (unsweetened)
Whole raw almonds

Add all of the smoothie ingredients to a blender and blend until smooth and creamy.

Smoothie bowl: Pour the blend into a bowl, then add toppings as desired.

Smoothie: Drink the blend immediately, refrigerate it in an airtight container for up to 24 hours, or freeze it in an airtight container until ready to use. If you prefer a thinner smoothie, stir in your choice of liquid until you achieve the desired consistency.

DAY 2

Breakfast
Eat a challenge-approved smoothie bowl.

AM Snack
Eat a healthy snack.
Example: Sliced banana with peanut butter.

Lunch
Eat a healthy lunch of your choice.
Example: Grilled chicken over garden greens.

PM Snack
Drink one 8- to 12-ounce challenge-approved acai smoothie.

Dinner
Eat a healthy meal of your choice.
Example: Salmon with roasted vegetables and quinoa.

Daily Habits
- Drink at least 8 glasses of water.
- Get at least 30 minutes of exercise.
- Practice mindfulness (like gratitude or meditation) once a day.

Today's Recommended Wellness-Challenge Recipe

Antioxidant Rush
Servings: 2

Base and Smoothie
1 packet frozen acai puree (unsweetened)
1 medium frozen banana
½ cup fresh blueberries
½ cup fresh strawberries
½ cup coconut water or chocolate almond milk
2 tablespoons chocolate protein powder (optional)
¼–½ cup preferred liquid to dilute (optional)

Suggested Bowl Toppings
Almond butter
Blueberries
Cacao nibs or dark chocolate shavings
Unsweetened coconut flakes

Base and Smoothie
1 packet frozen acai puree (unsweetened)
1 medium frozen banana
½ cup fresh or frozen mango
½ cup fresh or frozen pineapple
½ cup coconut water
¼–½ cup preferred liquid to dilute (optional)

Suggested Bowl Toppings
Almond butter
Banana slices
Low-fat granola
Mango cubes
Strawberry slices
Unsweetened coconut flakes

Add all of the smoothie ingredients to a blender and blend until smooth and creamy.

Smoothie bowl: Pour the blend into a bowl, then add toppings as desired.

Smoothie: Drink the blend immediately, refrigerate it in an airtight container for up to 24 hours, or freeze it in an airtight container until ready to use. If you prefer a thinner smoothie, stir in your choice of liquid until you achieve the desired consistency.

DAY 4

Breakfast
Eat a challenge-approved smoothie bowl.
AM Snack
Eat a healthy snack.
Example: Celery sticks with light cream cheese.

Lunch
Eat a healthy lunch of your choice.
Example: Crunchy chickpea and kale Caesar salad.

PM Snack

Drink one 8- to 12-ounce challenge-approved acai smoothie.

Dinner
Eat a healthy meal of your choice.
Example: Sheet pan roast chicken and veggies.

Daily Habits
- Drink at least 8 glasses of water.
- Get at least 30 minutes of exercise.
- Practice mindfulness (like gratitude or meditation) once a day.

Today's Recommended Wellness-Challenge Recipe

Peanut Butter Power
Servings: 2

Base and Smoothie
1 packet frozen acai puree (un-sweetened)
1 medium frozen banana
½ cup frozen strawberries
½ cup frozen blueberries
½ cup almond milk
2 rounded tablespoons creamy peanut butter
¼–½ cup preferred liquid to dilute (optional)

Suggested Bowl Toppings
Blueberries
Granola
Peanut butter
Strawberry slices
Unsweetened coconut flakes
Add all of the smoothie ingredients to a blender and blend until smooth and creamy.

Smoothie bowl: Pour the blend into a bowl, then add toppings as desired.

Smoothie: Drink the blend immediately, refrigerate it in an airtight container for up to 24 hours, or freeze it in an airtight container until ready to use. If you prefer a thinner smoothie, stir in your choice of liquid until you achieve the desired consistency.

DAY 5

Breakfast
Eat a challenge-approved smoothie bowl.

AM Snack
Eat a healthy snack.
Example: Cherry tomatoes with light mozzarella cheese.

Lunch
Eat a healthy lunch of your choice.
Example: Chicken and vegetable soup.

PM Snack
Drink one 8- to 12-ounce challenge-approved acai smoothie.

Dinner
Eat a healthy meal of your choice.
Example: Baked crab cakes with side salad.

Daily Habits
- Drink at least 8 glasses of water.
- Get at least 30 minutes of exercise.
- Practice mindfulness (like gratitude or meditation) once a day.

Today's Recommended Wellness-Challenge Recipe
Berry Good Smoothie Bowl
Servings: 2

Base and Smoothie
2 packets frozen acai puree (unsweetened)

1 medium frozen banana
1 cup frozen mixed berries
½ cup almond or cashew milk
2 tablespoons almond butter
¼–½ cup preferred liquid to dilute (optional)

Suggested Bowl Toppings
Cacao nibs or dark chocolate shavings
Chia seeds
Hemp seeds, optional
Mixed berries
Unsweetened coconut flakes

Add all of the smoothie ingredients to a blender and blend until smooth and creamy.

Smoothie bowl: Pour the blend into a bowl, then add toppings as desired.

Smoothie: Drink the blend immediately, refrigerate it in an airtight container for up to 24 hours, or freeze it in an airtight container until ready to use. If you prefer a thinner smoothie, stir in your choice of liquid until you achieve the desired consistency.

DAY 6

Breakfast
Eat a challenge-approved smoothie bowl.

AM Snack
Eat a healthy snack.
Example: A small bowl of healthy cereal without milk.

Lunch
Eat a healthy lunch of your choice.
Example: Harvest salad with butternut squash.

PM Snack
Drink one 8- to 12-ounce challenge-approved acai smoothie.

Dinner

Eat a healthy meal of your choice.
Example: Homemade chicken and broccoli stir-fry.

Daily Habits
- Drink at least 8 glasses of water.
- Get at least 30 minutes of exercise.
- Practice mindfulness (like gratitude or meditation) once a day.

Today's Recommended Wellness-Challenge Recipe

Balancing Blend
Servings: 2

Base and Smoothie
1 packet frozen acai puree (unsweetened)
1 medium frozen banana
1 cup frozen blueberries
½ cup frozen mango
¼ medium avocado
½ cup almond milk
1 teaspoon chia seeds
¼–½ cup preferred liquid to dilute (optional)

Suggested Bowl Toppings
Chopped almonds or hazelnuts
Kiwi slices
Low-fat granola
Mixed berries

Add all of the smoothie ingredients to a blender and blend until smooth and creamy.

Smoothie bowl: Pour the blend into a bowl, then add toppings as desired.

Smoothie: Drink the blend immediately, refrigerate it in an airtight container for up to 24 hours, or freeze it in an airtight container until ready to use. If you prefer a thinner smoothie, stir in your choice of liquid until you achieve the desired consistency.

DAY 7

Breakfast
Eat a challenge-approved smoothie bowl.

AM Snack
Eat a healthy snack.
Example: A simple-ingredient protein bar.

Lunch
Eat a healthy lunch of your choice.
Example: White chicken chili with avocado.

PM Snack
Drink one 8- to 12-ounce challenge-approved acai smoothie.

Dinner
Eat a healthy meal of your choice.
Example: Cilantro-lime shrimp wraps.

Daily Habits
- Drink at least 8 glasses of water.
- Get at least 30 minutes of exercise.
- Practice mindfulness (like gratitude or meditation) once a day.

Today's Recommended Wellness-Challenge Recipe

Simple Superfood Smoothie
Servings: 2

Base and Smoothie
1 packet frozen acai puree (unsweetened)
1 cup frozen mango
1 large ripe banana
1 cup unsweetened vanilla almond milk
¼–½ cup preferred liquid to dilute (optional)

Suggested Bowl Toppings
Banana slices
Blueberries
Hemp seeds
Pomegranate seeds

Unsweetened coconut flakes

Add all of the smoothie ingredients
to a blender and blend until smooth
and creamy.

Smoothie bowl: Pour the blend into
a bowl, then add toppings as desired.

Smoothie: Drink the blend immediately, refrigerate it in an airtight container for up to
24 hours, or freeze it in an airtight container until ready to use. If you prefer a thinner
smoothie, stir in your choice of liquid until you achieve the desired consistency.

DAY 8

Breakfast
Eat a challenge-approved smoothie bowl.

AM Snack
Eat a healthy snack.
Example: Sliced apple with 1 ounce of light cheddar cheese.

Lunch
Eat a healthy lunch of your choice.
Example: Chicken salad made with an avocado base.

PM Snack
Drink one 8- to 12-ounce challenge-approved acai smoothie.

Dinner
Eat a healthy meal of your choice.
Example: Roasted peppers stuffed with turkey, beans, and quinoa.

Daily Habits
- Drink at least 8 glasses of water.
- Get at least 30 minutes of exercise.
- Practice mindfulness (like gratitude or meditation) once a day.

Today's Recommended Wellness-Challenge Recipe

Green Power
Servings: 2

Base and Smoothie
¼ cup spinach (pre-blended)
1 packet frozen acai puree (unsweetened)
1 medium frozen banana
½ cup almond or coconut milk
½ cup canned coconut milk
¼ teaspoon pure vanilla extract
Pinch kosher salt
¼–½ cup preferred liquid to dilute (optional)

Suggested Bowl Toppings
Hemp seeds
Kiwi slices
Low-fat granola
Mixed berries
Pistachios

Add all of the smoothie ingredients to a blender and blend until smooth and creamy.

Smoothie bowl: Pour the blend into a bowl, then add toppings as desired.

Smoothie: Drink the blend immediately, refrigerate it in an airtight container for up to 24 hours, or freeze it in an airtight container until ready to use. If you prefer a thinner smoothie, stir in your choice of liquid until you achieve the desired consistency.

DAY 9

Breakfast
Eat a challenge-approved smoothie bowl.

AM Snack

Eat a healthy snack.
Example: A handful of roasted edamame.

Lunch
Eat a healthy lunch of your choice.
Example: Spicy tuna poke bowl.

PM Snack
Drink one 8- to 12-ounce challenge-approved acai smoothie.

Dinner
Eat a healthy meal of your choice.
Example: Cranberry-orange pork tenderloin with green beans.

Daily Habits
- Drink at least 8 glasses of water.
- Get at least 30 minutes of exercise.
- Practice mindfulness (like gratitude or meditation) once a day.

Today's Recommended Wellness-Challenge Recipe

Sweet Support
Servings: 2

Base and Smoothie
1 packet frozen acai puree (unsweetened)
½ medium frozen banana
½ cup blueberries
½ cup frozen mango
½ cup frozen pineapple
½ cup frozen strawberries
½–1 cup almond milk
1 tablespoon honey
¼–½ cup preferred liquid to dilute (optional)

Suggested Bowl Toppings
Banana slices
Strawberry slices
Blueberries
Granola with almonds

Dark chocolate shavings
Unsweetened coconut flakes

Add all of the smoothie ingredients to a blender and blend until smooth and creamy.

Smoothie bowl: Pour the blend into a bowl, then add toppings as desired.

Smoothie: Drink the blend immediately, refrigerate it in an airtight container for up to 24 hours, or freeze it in an airtight container until ready to use. If you prefer a thinner smoothie, stir in your choice of liquid until you achieve the desired consistency.

DAY 10

Breakfast
Eat a challenge-approved smoothie bowl.

AM Snack
Eat a healthy snack.
Example: Homemade no-bake energy bites.

Lunch
Eat a healthy lunch of your choice.
Example: Loaded vegetarian baked sweet potato.

PM Snack
Drink one 8- to 12-ounce challenge-approved acai smoothie.

Dinner
Eat a healthy meal of your choice.
Example: Zucchini noodles with chicken, cherry tomatoes, and pesto.

Daily Habits
- Drink at least 8 glasses of water.
- Get at least 30 minutes of exercise.
- Practice mindfulness (like gratitude or meditation) once a day.

Today's Recommended Wellness-Challenge Recipe

Chocolate Nourishment
Servings: 2

Base and Smoothie
2 packets frozen acai puree (unsweetened)
1 cup frozen cherries or mixed berries
1 medium frozen banana
1 tablespoon cacao powder
½ cup chocolate almond milk
¼–½ cup preferred liquid to dilute (optional)

Suggested Bowl Toppings
Cacao nibs or dark chocolate shavings
Chopped almonds
Drizzle of honey
Low-fat granola
Raspberries
Strawberry slices
Unsweetened coconut flakes

Add all of the smoothie ingredients to a blender and blend until smooth and creamy.

Smoothie bowl: Pour the blend into a bowl, then add toppings as desired.

Smoothie: Drink the blend immediately, refrigerate it in an airtight container for up to 24 hours, or freeze it in an airtight container until ready to use. If you prefer a thinner smoothie, stir in your choice of liquid until you achieve the desired consistency.

The Four Pillars of the Perfect Wellness Routine

Healthy living doesn't have to involve some complicated combination of calorie counting, heartrate monitoring, and macrobiotic cooking. The best wellness routine is a simple wellness routine. As long as you incorporate these four basics—nourishing food, regular exercise, plenty of water, and rest—you're well on your way to wellness. Each day of the

10-Day Acai-Powered Wellness Challenge combines the magic of acai with these four essentials to help you create good habits that will last you a long, healthy lifetime.

BALANCE

Man cannot live on smoothie bowls alone, if only because salmon and broccoli make for poor toppings. Smoothies and smoothie bowls are an essential part of your wellness challenge—they cram a ton of nutrients into a small, addictively delicious package. But your body needs even more variety than a smoothie bowl can offer. (Your mind needs the variety, too. Nothing tests your will to eat healthy like boredom.)

Just like acai is one powerful ingredient in a smoothie, smoothies are one powerful ingredient in the recipe for good health. For you to feel your best, you'll need to balance out your acai intake with whole grains, protein-rich foods, and a variety of vegetables. The more diversity you have in your healthy meals, the better your body will function.

MOVEMENT

If the only times you move your body are to go from your desk chair to your car seat to your couch, you'll never feel the full benefits of acai. Regular exercise is an integral part of your overall wellness. Not only does it help your body metabolize nutrients so that you *are* well, it also helps you *feel* well by giving you strength and energy.

Getting regular exercise doesn't mean you have to run out and join a CrossFit club. Move your body in whatever way you like, whether that's yoga flow or a 5K run. Not sure what that looks like? Just keep trying different forms of exercise until you find one or two that you can look forward to doing, then aim to do them for about 30 minutes every day. And if you can, get some fresh air while you're at it. The natural light and vitamin D will amplify the mental and physical health benefits of your exercise.

HYDRATION

You know that you're supposed to be drinking at least eight glasses of water each day, but you might not know why. Water doesn't just quell your cotton mouth—it helps your body absorb nutrients and flush out toxins. Without proper hydration, none of that acai superfood goodness will make it to your brain, heart, stomach, or skin. And downing a gallon just once a day so you don't forget won't help. Your body needs gradual hydration.

Having a smoothie bowl in the morning, a smoothie in the afternoon, and plenty of fruits and vegetables in between can definitely help you get the hydration you need. But the more you get, the better you're going to feel and look. So use an app if you have to, but make sure you're getting your eight glasses a day.

REST
If you're like most people, you probably don't get enough rest. That includes not just restful sleep, but also downtime. It's so easy to spend your day mindlessly scrolling through work emails, text messages, and social media feeds that you don't even notice you never gave your brain a proper break. That's why mindfulness is built right into your challenge.

Try to spend *at least* ten minutes per day practicing some sort of mindfulness technique to help your brain and your body reset. This could be meditation, journaling, or even just sitting quietly and taking a few deep breaths. Then, make sure you leave room in your schedule for at least 7 consecutive hours of sleep each night. (Set a "turn off the TV" alarm if you have to!) After ten days of getting enough rest, you'll feel like a whole new you.

Make the Most of It
Whether the word "challenge" gets your blood pumping or makes your stomach flutter, you picked up this book and made the decision to do your best for these ten days. And you'll be so happy you did! Once you get a taste of acai-powered wellness, you'll never go back to feeling "blah." So, are you ready to squeeze every last drop of goodness out of this experience? Just follow these tips, and you'll be well on your way to creating the healthy life you crave.

DIP YOUR TOES
Have you ever made a smoothie before? Do you have healthy dinner recipes on hand? What kind of exercise do you like? These are a few of the things you'll want to sort out before you start the 10-Day Acai-Powered Wellness Challenge in earnest. Try out a few smoothie recipes and styles of exercise to learn what you like and get used to how they affect your days. Then, a few days before you begin, start a lite version of the challenge: drink one smoothie a day and make time for a few minutes of movement. In other words, get used to the water before you dive in.

DON'T OVERDO IT
Creamy, fruity smoothie blends can be addictive. Not only are they delicious, they're also good for you. So why not eat them all day long? Because you *can* have too much of a good thing—especially when that good thing is full of natural sugars. Plus, consuming

too much fiber (prevalent in fruits and veggies) can cause digestive upset, especially if you're not used to it. Just stick to the challenge's recommended two servings of smoothie blends per day, and give your body time to adjust to its new routine. You'll get all of the goodness without any unpleasant side effects.

FOLLOW THE FRAMEWORK
The beautiful thing about the 10-Day Acai-Powered Wellness Challenge is that it's completely customizable. Do what you need to do to make it work for you—as long as you follow the framework. Each piece of the plan (and its timing) is designed for optimal wellness. The morning smoothie bowl gives you the energy you need to start your day, while the snack that follows creates complete proteins and helps you absorb acai's vitamins and minerals. Two more balanced meals give your body the nutrients it needs, while an afternoon smoothie maximizes your acai intake and encourages hydration. If you want to feel your best on Day 10, checking off all the daily challenge boxes is key.

GO EASY ON THE SWEET STUFF
When it comes to your morning smoothie bowl, it's easy to get carried away. There are just so many toppings to choose from! But you want to choose ingredients that let the sweetness of the fruit shine—and that don't add to the sugar content of the bowl. Many of your favorite ingredients, from the acai itself to the coconut flakes, can contain added sugar. Check labels for hidden sugars (like honey, agave, fructose, or sucrose) or the words "no sugar added." It's okay if you prefer sweetened coconut or semi-sweet chocolate chips. Just make sure you're mindful of how much sugar makes it into your breakfast bowl.

MAKE IT WORK FOR YOU
Life doesn't stop because you challenge yourself to get healthy, so you have to make the challenge fit into your life. If a recipe suggestion isn't your cup of tea or you don't have time for that morning jog, avoid the temptation to just fall back on bad habits. That might mean scouring healthy cookbooks to find go-to recipes you're excited about, or streaming a yoga video before bed instead of getting up early. It could also be as simple as swapping out banana for mango in your smoothie bowl. Remember, this plan was designed to *empower* you to transform your health. Take what it gives you and run with it!

FOCUS ON PROGRESS, NOT PERFECTION
Building good habits isn't always easy, especially if you're making big changes to your usual routine. Be patient with yourself during your challenge. If you're desperate for a full-fat caramel latte, don't deprive yourself. That's a recipe for the kind of resentment

that leads to giving up entirely. Trying to be perfect is a losing game, and a tedious one at that. Just focus on feeling well and doing better today than you did yesterday. Of course, this doesn't mean that you can just throw all of your good habits on top of the bad ones. Stick to the plan as much as possible, and simply forgive yourself for any slip-ups.

PRIORITIZE SLEEP

Superfood smoothies are incredibly beneficial, but they can't counteract the effects of sleep deprivation, which can take a serious toll on your health. Without enough downtime, toxins can build up in your body and lead to things like anxiety, high blood pressure, and obesity. So, if you really want to be well and feel great, you need to make sleep a priority. That means setting a schedule and sticking to it so that you can get between 7 and 9 hours of sleep each night. Set an alarm to remind you to wind down about an hour before bedtime, and avoid screens during that hour. If you still have trouble drifting off, download an app that offers breathing exercises and soothing "bedtime stories." They may seem silly, but they work.

VISUALIZE THE RESULTS

Before you begin the challenge, take a few minutes to decide what you want to get out of it. Do you want to have more energy? Lose a few pounds? Set yourself up for good health in the long-term? Getting clear on your goals can help you stick to the plan and meet them. Every morning during the challenge, remind yourself of what you hope to gain from the experience. But don't just think about your goals, visualize the results. Picture yourself feeling energized, healthy, and trim. And every day, celebrate your wins—things like making a beautiful smoothie bowl, eating a well-rounded meal, and taking a 30-minute walk. By fulling embracing the challenge, you'll get even more out of it.

SAVOR THE FRESH FLAVORS

When you're used to fast food, frozen dinners, or sweet treats, using any sort of meal plan can seem daunting. The phrase "health food" conjures up a frightening image of small plates and flavorless steamed food. But remember, the 10-Day Acai-Powered Wellness Challenge isn't a diet or a detox. Not only will you be enjoying delicious smoothie blends, you'll also have complete control over your menu. If you're craving Asian takeout, look for a healthy copycat recipe. Need mac and cheese now? You'd be amazed what you can do with cauliflower. Create blends and recipes with your favorite flavors, then take the time to really enjoy them and appreciate what you're doing for your health.

Great Expectations

During the 10-Day Acai-Powered Wellness Challenge, you're going to transform the way you look and feel. Powerful nutrients, thoughtful movement, and mindful moments combine to give you more energy, better digestion, improved mindset, and clearer skin. Keep up the good work beyond those first ten days, and the rewards are even greater. Your healthy new habits could help you lose weight, protect your heart, boost your brain function, and even avoid chronic illness and cancer. When you make transformational changes like these, you can expect a few growing pains. Be patient and remember what you're working toward. Day 10 is worth it!

MORE ENERGY

Spending ten days fueling your body with whole, healthful foods like acai and regular exercise could have you feeling years younger, especially if you weren't taking great care of yourself before the challenge. Energizing benefits of a balanced diet include a bevy of B vitamins, fatty acids, protein, and fiber. Combined with movement and mindfulness, these nutrients should also boost your mood, which will have you feeling even more invigorated. Just remember that it's going to take more than enjoying a single smoothie bowl to start seeing results, and your body will need time to adjust to your new routine. So don't be discouraged if you notice a small dip in your energy reserves at first. After a few days, those reserves will be overflowing.

BETTER DIGESTION

A balanced diet full of fiber and antioxidants is just what the doctor ordered to improve your digestion. Not only can that help you feel great, it can also help give you a leaner stomach so you look great! You may notice a bit of gas and bloating while your body adjusts to the amount of fiber in your diet. Make sure that you're drinking plenty of water, which will help reduce any negative effects. Once you get used to your new routine, that same fiber will help improve your digestion and *reduce* the amount of gas and bloating you experience.

IMPROVED MINDSET

You might be surprised to discover how much your physical wellness can affect your mental health. When you make poor food choices or spend your days sitting, you might feel sluggish and unmotivated. The 10-Day Acai-Powered Wellness Challenge is about to change that. Combine an antioxidant-rich, acai-centered diet with regular exercise and a mindfulness practice, and you're bound to find yourself in a better mood. But you're human, so it would be completely understandable if you got a little grouchy from missing your favorite treats. Switching your focus from food to experiences might help. Instead of going out for a rich dinner, invite a friend to join you for a healthy meal and an evening walk. It won't be long before scrumptious acai smoothies *become* your favorite treat.

CLEARER SKIN

Completing the 10-Day Acai-Powered Wellness Challenge is a great way to get a clear, glowing complexion. You'll be skipping added sugars, processed foods, and red meat, all of which can clog pores. And your diet will be filled with skin-loving vitamins, minerals, and antioxidants. Over time, those antioxidants may even help you reduce the appearance of wrinkles and sun damage.

If acne is of special concern for you, you should tailor the challenge to your troublesome skin. First, replace all dairy milk and milk products (known acne triggers) with nondairy alternatives. Then commit to a simple skincare routine that involves regular cleansing and moisturizing, being careful to choose products that work well with your skin. After the challenge, reintroduce potential triggers to your diet one at a time, taking a few days to see whether any new acne crops up. People who are prone to acne (and even some who aren't) may experience a purge phase, where your body expels toxins through your pores. Keep the faith and give the challenge time to work its magic. As soon as the toxins are out of your system, your skin will look better than ever!

Day 11

You did it! You conquered the 10-Day Acai-Powered Wellness Challenge, and you should celebrate your success. And what better way to celebrate than to continue feeling nourished and energized? You've already laid the foundation for developing healthy habits that could last you a lifetime. Make the most of that momentum by completing another ten days. And another ten after that. Before you know it, feeling amazing will be your new normal.

Now that you have the hang of things, you can make changes to the challenge and incorporate more of what you love. And you can experiment with the endless variety of delicious acai smoothie blends that exist in the world. Starting on the next page, you'll find fifty mouthwatering recipes for all of your health-improvement needs. And those are just to get you started. Once you're comfortable enough, you can use the information under "Powerful Partners" (starting on page 33) to create acai-powered blends tailored just to you.

PART 4

Smoothie and Smoothie Bowl Recipes

Recipes for Wellness

Congratulations on completing the 10-Day Acai-Powered Wellness Challenge! You took your well-being into your own hands and laid the foundation for a lifetime of good health, and that's something to be proud of. Now that you've had a taste of what real nourishment feels like (a.k.a., amazing), are you ready to make acai a regular part of your routine?

Think about how you'll feel a year from now, knowing that you're feeding your body what it needs to thrive. Imagine feeling even more energized and uplifted. Visualize that strong heartbeat, see that glowing skin. It's all within reach, when you embrace the power of acai. And this is the perfect place to start.

The following pages contain fifty delicious acai-centered recipes for you to try. These blends are organized by their best health benefits, from antioxidant-rich anti-aging mixes to superfood powerhouses for whole-body wellness. But don't let the sectioning keep you from trying them all—like acai itself, these recipes are multitaskers. Every one of them will bring you closer to your wellness goals.

Thanks to the 10-day challenge, you're already starting to understand what you like in an acai blend. The more recipes you try, the more you'll discover what works for you (and what doesn't). Don't be afraid to make these recipes your own, just like you did during the challenge. Make substitutions, alter amounts, and create different flavor combinations. Then, once you hit your smoothie-making stride, use the information you learned in "Powerful Partners" (starting on page 33) to design your own healthful blends. The sky's the limit!

If you need a refresher on the blending process, turn to page 21. Otherwise, just keep these guidelines in mind:

- **Use the best.** Remember, whatever goes into the blender goes into your body. Always start with high-quality, organic produce. Then make sure you wash your ingredients well (including the frozen ones) and properly prep them (i.e., remove anything you don't want to eat, like stems). You can strain out blackberry seeds, but you can't strain out bacteria or pesticides, so better safe than sorry!
- **Make it yours.** The great thing about smoothies and smoothie bowls is that they're flexible. Use the flavors and toppings that speak to you! The trick is to

swap out items with ones of a similar consistency. (Think: frozen banana for frozen avocado or fresh mango for fresh strawberries.) Taste the blend before you pour it, then make any necessary adjustments.

- **Pick and choose.** Each smoothie-bowl recipe contains a list of suggested toppings, and they're just that: suggestions. You don't have to add everything on the list. In fact, you don't have to add any of them. You can swap out the toppings for ones you prefer, or even just drink the blend as a smoothie.
- **Switch it up.** Wish that smoothie recipe was fit for a bowl? Easy! Just reduce the amount of liquid you use and add toppings. Or turn a bowl into a drinkable smoothie by adding up to ½ cup of whatever liquid you like.
- **Drink it fresh.** Although using frozen ingredients can help your smoothie "keep" longer, you'll still want to drink your blend as soon as possible. The fresher the blend, the more nutrients it holds. If you can't drink your smoothie immediately, refrigerate it in an airtight container for up to 24 hours, or freeze it in an airtight container until you're ready for it.
- **Don't go crazy.** During the 10-Day Acai-Powered Wellness Challenge, you enjoyed small servings so that your body could get used to its new routine. For many of the recipes in this section, however, a serving size could be a tall glass. Just be mindful of your daily intake. Smoothies may be a very convenient way to pack in the superfoods, but they can also be calorie bombs if you're not careful. Make sure you enjoy smoothie bowls (and their many scrumptious toppings) in moderation, and don't be tempted to substitute a smoothie for every meal. A healthy diet is a balanced one.

That about covers it, but here are just a few more ingredient-specific tips that might come in handy as you perfect your blends:

- **Not a fan of bananas?** Thanks to its creamy consistency, banana is one of the most common smoothie ingredients around. If you're not wild about bananas, though, you can sub in an alternative thickener. A few of these include finely ground oatmeal, avocado, frozen mango or peach slices, and Greek yogurt.
- **Want to add oatmeal?** Dry oats can make a great bowl topping, but you might not want to slurp them through a straw. When using oatmeal in a blend, add it to the blender before adding other ingredients and grind it into a fine powder. Once everything is blended, let the mixture set for up to 24 hours in an airtight container in the fridge so that the oats can soak up some of the liquid and thicken up.
- **Crazy for chia seeds?** When you mix chia seeds with liquid, they create a gel.

That's why mixing dry chia seeds into a smoothie can sometimes make it feel a little strange. For the best texture, let the seeds gel up in liquid for a few minutes before adding them to your blend, and make sure you don't add more than 1 tablespoon per serving.

There are just so many wonderful ways to enjoy the amazing flavors and health benefits of acai-powered blends. Why wait another minute? Jump right in and try a few!

AGING

Avocado Glow Skin Smoothie

Ready to simplify your anti-aging efforts? Skip the 10-step skincare routine and get glowing from the inside out. This dairy- and sugar-free blend is loaded with skin-loving antioxidants and amino acids. Plus, avocado offers up a healthy dose of vitamin E (a well-known guardian of great skin) while making your smoothie extra creamy and delightful.

Servings: 1–2

Ingredients:
1 packet frozen acai puree (unsweetened)
1 medium frozen banana
½ medium avocado
1½ cups coconut water
½ cup unsweetened almond milk
1 teaspoon coconut oil

Add all the ingredients to a blender and blend until smooth and creamy. Drink the smoothie immediately, refrigerate it in an airtight container for up to 24 hours, or freeze it in an airtight container until you are ready to drink it.

Blueberry-Pomegranate Bliss

Leave it to nature to fortify two of its best-tasting beauties with powerful antioxidant properties! Blueberry and pomegranate are the stars of this bowl—not just because they're delicious, but also because they are anti-aging powerhouses. Top your bowl with kiwi and berries for an extra dose of clarifying vitamin C, and you'll be well on your way to turning back time.

Servings: 2

Ingredients:
Smoothie Bowl Base
1 packet frozen acai puree (unsweetened)
1 medium frozen banana
1 cup frozen blueberries
1 cup fresh or frozen pomegranate seeds
½ cup almond milk or coconut water

Suggested Bowl Toppings
Chia seeds
Fresh berries
Kiwi slices
Pomegranate seeds
Unsweetened coconut flakes

Add all the smoothie ingredients to a blender and blend until smooth and creamy. Pour the blend into a bowl, then add toppings as desired.

To use this blend for a smoothie, skip the toppings and add ¼–½ cup of whatever liquid you like to dilute the blend to your preferred consistency for drinking. Drink the smoothie immediately, refrigerate it in an airtight container for up to 24 hours, or freeze it in an airtight container until you are ready to drink it.

Coconut Skin Quencher

Antioxidant-rich ingredients are a no-brainer when you're trying to stop the aging process in its tracks, but there's an even more essential piece of the puzzle: hydration. This blend is packed with powerful thirst-quenching ingredients, from blueberries and coconut water to spinach and hemp seeds. And don't worry—you won't even know the spinach is there!

Servings: 2

Ingredients:
1 packed cup baby spinach, pre-blended
1 packet frozen acai puree (unsweetened)
2 medium frozen bananas
1 cup fresh or frozen blueberries
½ cup fresh or frozen pomegranate seeds
1 tablespoon hemp seeds
½–1 cup coconut water

Add all the ingredients to a blender and blend until smooth and creamy. Drink the smoothie immediately, refrigerate it in an airtight container for up to 24 hours, or freeze it in an airtight container until you are ready to drink it.

ALLERGIES

Blueberry-Pineapple Allergy Protection

If you're especially sensitive to allergy season, this is the smoothie bowl for you. It avoids potential triggers like bananas and strawberries but includes a secret weapon: pineapple. Bromelain, an enzyme in pineapple, can reduce nasal swelling and make it easier to breathe. Top your smoothie bowls off with a drizzle of local honey or a spoonful of bee pollen to help desensitize you to local allergens.

Servings: 1–2

Ingredients:
Smoothie Bowl Base
1 packet frozen acai puree (unsweetened)
1 cup frozen pineapple
¼ cup frozen blueberries
2 tablespoons sunflower or nut butter
¼–½ cup coconut milk
1–2 scoops vanilla protein powder (optional)

Suggested Bowl Toppings
Local honey and/or bee pollen
Blueberries
Pineapple
Sunflower or nut butter
Unsweetened coconut flakes

Add all the smoothie ingredients to a blender and blend until smooth and creamy. Pour the blend into a bowl, then add toppings as desired.

To use this blend for a smoothie, skip the toppings and add ¼–½ cup of whatever liquid you like to dilute the blend to your preferred consistency for drinking. Drink the smoothie immediately, refrigerate it in an airtight container for up to 24 hours, or freeze it in an airtight container until you are ready to drink it.

Ginger-Lime Airway Opener

You can't do anything about allergens in the air, but you can do something about the inflammation they cause. For one thing, you can drink this smoothie, which is rich in anti-inflammatory ingredients that will help you breathe easier. Plus, the vitamin C found in lime and acai acts as a natural antihistamine.

Servings: 2

Ingredients:
1 packet frozen acai puree (unsweetened)
2 medium fresh or frozen bananas
Juice of ½–1 medium lime
1 (1-inch) piece ginger, peeled
½ cup coconut water
2 tablespoons aloe vera gel
1 pinch kosher salt

Add all the ingredients to a blender and blend until smooth and creamy. Drink the smoothie immediately, refrigerate it in an airtight container for up to 24 hours, or freeze it in an airtight container until you are ready to drink it.

Edible Antihistamine

In case the mouthwatering flavors in this tropical-style bowl aren't enough to entice you to try it, it also packs in powerful allergy-fighting properties. The omega-3 fatty acids in nuts and flaxseeds fight hay fever, the vitamin C in berries and kiwi act as a natural antihistamine, and the digestive enzymes in kefir and yogurt reduce the inflammation that causes allergic symptoms. Not bad for one little bowl! (But also, it does taste amazing.)

Servings: 2

Ingredients:
Smoothie Bowl Base
1 packet frozen acai puree (unsweetened)
1 medium frozen banana
½ cup fresh or frozen strawberries
½ cup fresh or frozen kiwi slices
½ cup full-fat kefir or Greek-style yogurt
¼–½ cup coconut water (optional, for consistency)

Suggested Bowl Toppings
Chopped walnuts or almonds
Flaxseeds
Fresh berries
Kiwi slices
Unsweetened coconut flakes

Add all the smoothie ingredients to a blender and blend until smooth and creamy. Pour the blend into a bowl, then add toppings as desired.

To use this blend for a smoothie, skip the toppings and add ¼–½ cup of whatever liquid you like to dilute the blend to your preferred consistency for drinking. Drink the smoothie immediately, refrigerate it in an airtight container for up to 24 hours, or freeze it in an airtight container until you are ready to drink it.

BEAUTY

"Green" Detox Smoothie

Make your gut happy and your skin will follow. Why? Because toxins need somewhere to go—if they're not eliminated through your digestive tract, they can show up in your skin. This detox blend uses a combination of antioxidants, protein, fiber, and fatty acids to make your whole body happy. Don't let the spinach fool you—this isn't your ordinary green juice. Although it offers the same sensible benefits, it feels like a tasty treat.

Servings: 2

Ingredients:
2 cups fresh baby spinach, pre-blended
1 packet frozen acai puree (unsweetened)
2 medium fresh or frozen bananas
2 tablespoons collagen powder
2 tablespoons chia seeds
1½ cups unsweetened almond milk

Add all the ingredients to a blender and blend until smooth and creamy. Drink the smoothie immediately, refrigerate it in an airtight container for up to 24 hours, or freeze it in an airtight container until you are ready to drink it.

Ube Beauty Boost

If you've never had ube, now is the time. These beautiful rich-purple vegetables are a staple in the Philippines, and for good reason. They're bursting with vitamins, minerals, and antioxidants. This beautifying blend combines ube's nutrients and gentle, nutty flavor with other skin-loving ingredients, such as collagen, kiwi, and figs.

Servings: 1

Ingredients:
Smoothie Bowl Base
1 packet frozen acai puree (unsweetened)
1 medium frozen banana
1 medium ube (purple yam)
½ cup coconut water
1 tablespoon collagen powder

Suggested Bowl Toppings
Chia seeds
Kiwi slices
Fig halves
Cacao nibs or dark chocolate shavings
Unsweetened coconut flakes

Add all the smoothie ingredients to a blender and blend until smooth and creamy. Pour the blend into a bowl, then add toppings as desired.

To use this blend for a smoothie, skip the toppings and add ¼–½ cup of whatever liquid you like to dilute the blend to your preferred consistency for drinking. Drink the smoothie immediately, refrigerate it in an airtight container for up to 24 hours, or freeze it in an airtight container until you are ready to drink it.

Cashew-Collagen Beauty Blend

A great way to get glowing skin is to give your body the fuel it needs and get out of its way. This bowl does just that by packing in flavor and nutrients without any skin-clogging sugar or dairy. Adding a tablespoon of collagen to the mix all but guarantees healthy hair, skin, and nails.

Servings: 1

Ingredients:
Smoothie Bowl Base
1 packet frozen acai puree (unsweetened)
1 medium frozen banana
2 medium dates, pitted and chopped
1 rounded tablespoon cashew butter
½–1 cup cashew milk
1 tablespoon collagen powder (optional)

Suggested Bowl Toppings
Cashew butter
Cinnamon
Fresh berries
Granola

Add all the smoothie ingredients to a blender and blend until smooth and creamy. Pour the blend into a bowl, then add toppings as desired.

To use this blend for a smoothie, skip the toppings and add ¼–½ cup of whatever liquid you like to dilute the blend to your preferred consistency for drinking. Drink the smoothie immediately, refrigerate it in an airtight container for up to 24 hours, or freeze it in an airtight container until you are ready to drink it.

BLOOD SUGAR

Sweet Satisfaction Blood Sugar Bowl

Watching your blood sugar doesn't mean giving up all things sweet. This brilliant blend will keep you feeling full *and* satisfy your sweet tooth with low-glycemic ingredients, which means no post-bowl blood-sugar crashes.

Servings: 1

Ingredients:
Smoothie Bowl Base
1 packet frozen acai puree (unsweetened)
1 medium frozen banana
¼ cup coconut water

Suggested Bowl Toppings
Almond butter
Banana slices
Chia seeds
Raw sunflower seeds
Strawberry slices

Add all the smoothie ingredients to a blender and blend until smooth and creamy. Pour the blend into a bowl, then add toppings as desired.

To use this blend for a smoothie, skip the toppings and add ¼ ½ cup of whatever liquid you like to dilute the blend to your preferred consistency for drinking. Drink the smoothie immediately, refrigerate it in an airtight container for up to 24 hours, or freeze it in an airtight container until you are ready to drink it.

Banana-Free Berry Blend

This banana-free blend is a great way to treat yourself to great nutrition while managing your blood sugar. Not only are the berries in this superfood smoothie low glycemic, they're also brimming with the antioxidants, fiber, and phytochemicals that help reduce your risk of developing diseases like diabetes. If the texture of berry seeds bothers you, just pour your blend through a fine-mesh strainer before drinking it.

Servings: 2

Ingredients:
3 leaves kale, pre-blended
1 packet frozen acai puree (unsweetened)
1 cup frozen blackberries
1 cup frozen blueberries
1 cup frozen raspberries
2 cups unsweetened coconut water
2 tablespoons ground flaxseed

Add all the ingredients to a blender and blend until smooth and creamy. Drink the smoothie immediately, refrigerate it in an airtight container for up to 24 hours, or freeze it in an airtight container until you are ready to drink it.

Triple-A Balancing Blend

This delightfully creamy smoothie bowl combines acai, avocado, and almonds for a blend that will balance your blood sugar, keep your heart healthy, and give you the sustained energy you need to tackle anything. Want to make this bowl a staple? Freeze ripe avocado quarters in individual bags so that you always have one on hand.

Servings: 1

Ingredients:
Smoothie Bowl Base
1 large handful spinach, pre-blended
1 packet frozen acai puree (unsweetened)
½ medium frozen banana
1 cup frozen strawberries
¼ medium avocado
½ cup almond milk
1–2 tablespoons flaxseed meal

Suggested Bowl Toppings
Almond butter
Avocado slices
Chia seeds
Fresh berries
Hemp seeds

Add all the smoothie ingredients to a blender and blend until smooth and creamy. Pour the blend into a bowl, then add toppings as desired.

To use this blend for a smoothie, skip the toppings and add ¼–½ cup of whatever liquid you like to dilute the blend to your preferred consistency for drinking. Drink the smoothie immediately, refrigerate it in an airtight container for up to 24 hours, or freeze it in an airtight container until you are ready to drink it.

BONE HEALTH

Raspberry Bone Builder

To build strong bones, you need to work from the inside. This fresh blend has everything you need—calcium, potassium, protein, magnesium, and more. Raspberries are the secret weapon, though. They contain manganese, a trace mineral that's essential for bone health. For an even stronger smoothie, look for almond milk that's fortified with calcium and vitamin D.

Servings: 1

Ingredients:
1 packet frozen acai puree (unsweetened)
½ medium frozen banana
½ cup fresh or frozen raspberries
½ cup sliced zucchini
½ cup almond milk
2 tablespoons almond butter

Add all the ingredients to a blender and blend until smooth and creamy. Drink the smoothie immediately, refrigerate it in an airtight container for up to 24 hours, or freeze it in an airtight container until you are ready to drink it.

Blueberry-Mango Bone Defense

Want to know the secret to warding off fractures and breaks? Good nutrition. Luckily, this blend contains plenty of that, with ingredients rich in calcium, copper, iron, magnesium, manganese, and potassium—all essential elements of bone. Make sure you top it off with figs, which contain bone-building calcium, vitamin C, and vitamin K.

Servings: 1

Ingredients:
Smoothie Bowl Base
1 packet frozen acai puree (unsweetened)
1 large ripe banana
½ cup frozen blueberries
½ cup frozen mango
½–¾ cup unsweetened almond milk

Suggested Bowl Toppings
Banana slices
Cacao nibs
Fig halves
Fresh berries
Hemp hearts
Toasted coconut flakes

Add all the smoothie ingredients to a blender and blend until smooth and creamy. Pour the blend into a bowl, then add toppings as desired.

To use this blend for a smoothie, skip the toppings and add ¼–½ cup of whatever liquid you like to dilute the blend to your preferred consistency for drinking. Drink the smoothie immediately, refrigerate it in an airtight container for up to 24 hours, or freeze it in an airtight container until you are ready to drink it.

Summertime Strength Smoothie Bowl

Now you can build strong bones while enjoying a sweet, sunny treat! Not only will the flavors of pineapple, mango, and raspberries brighten your day, the fruits themselves will fill you up with nutrients that are essential to bone health. Enjoy these fresh summertime flavors year-round by buying produce at its peak and freezing it in chunks and slices to use later.

Servings: 1

Ingredients:

Smoothie Bowl Base

1 packet frozen acai puree (unsweetened)
1 cup frozen mango
1 teaspoon vanilla extract
¾ cup plain nonfat Greek yogurt
¼ cup almond milk

Suggested Bowl Toppings
Chia seeds
Chopped almonds
Pineapple
Raspberries
Unsweetened coconut flakes

Add all the smoothie ingredients to a blender and blend until smooth and creamy. Pour the blend into a bowl, then add toppings as desired.

To use this blend for a smoothie, skip the toppings and add ¼–½ cup of whatever liquid you like to dilute the blend to your preferred consistency for drinking. Drink the smoothie immediately, refrigerate it in an airtight container for up to 24 hours, or freeze it in an airtight container until you are ready to drink it.

BRAIN HEALTH

Antioxidant-Rich Avocado Smoothie

Are you the reigning champ of trivia night? There's no better blend than this one to get blood flowing to your brain—the healthy fats in avocado help you do just that. Plus, the omega-3 fatty acids in chia seeds build and repair brain cells while the antioxidants in acai, blueberries, and pomegranates protect against memory loss. Make this smoothie a regular part of your routine, and you're sure to keep your title.

Servings: 1

Ingredients:
1 packet frozen acai puree (unsweetened)
1 medium frozen banana
¾ cup fresh or frozen blueberries
¼ cup pomegranate seeds
½ medium avocado
½ cup almond milk
1 tablespoon chia seeds

Add all the ingredients to a blender and blend until smooth and creamy. Drink the smoothie immediately, refrigerate it in an airtight container for up to 24 hours, or freeze it in an airtight container until you are ready to drink it.

Berry-Chocolate Brain Boost

Antioxidant-rich berries and dark chocolate protect your brain from oxidative stress, but cherries are the real star of this bowl. Their anthocyanins and polyphenols have been shown to improve cognitive function, prevent memory loss, and even ward off Alzheimer's. And if that's not enough of a reason to eat chocolate for breakfast, both the flavors and the nutrients in this bowl can put you in a better mood.

Servings: 2

Ingredients:
Smoothie Bowl Base
2 packets frozen acai puree (unsweetened)
1 medium frozen banana
1 cup frozen cherries
1 tablespoon cacao powder
½ cup almond or chocolate almond milk

Suggested Bowl Toppings
Chopped almonds
Dark chocolate shavings
Fresh berries
Granola
Unsweetened coconut flakes

Add all the smoothie ingredients to a blender and blend until smooth and creamy. Pour the blend into a bowl, then add toppings as desired.

To use this blend for a smoothie, skip the toppings and add ¼–½ cup of whatever liquid you like to dilute the blend to your preferred consistency for drinking. Drink the smoothie immediately, refrigerate it in an airtight container for up to 24 hours, or freeze it in an airtight container until you are ready to drink it.

Goji Berry Brain Blend

Every inch of this blend works toward better brain function, from the mood-boosting nutrients in bananas to the fatty acids in coconut oil and hemp seeds that protect your ability to learn and remember. Blueberries and acai bring the antioxidants while goji berries help you produce choline to fend off neurological degeneration. Even apple juice can improve your memory! So, the next time you feel a brain fog rolling in, reach for this easy-but-essential blend.

Servings: 1

Ingredients:
1 packet frozen acai puree (unsweetened)
½ medium frozen banana
½ cup frozen blueberries
2 tablespoons dried goji berries
1 cup unsweetened apple juice
2 tablespoons hemp seeds
1 teaspoon coconut oil

Add all the ingredients to a blender and blend until smooth and creamy. Drink the smoothie immediately, refrigerate it in an airtight container for up to 24 hours, or freeze it in an airtight container until you are ready to drink it.

DIGESTION

Happy Gut Smoothie Bowl

Whether your stomach's a little unsettled or you're just trying to keep things moving, this blend has everything you need. Each ingredient was carefully chosen to contribute soluble fiber, probiotics, or anti-inflammatory properties, all of which contribute to healthy, balanced digestion. And with flavors like dark chocolate and coconut, your taste buds will be just as happy as your tummy.

Servings: 2

Ingredients:
Smoothie Bowl Base
¼ cup old-fashioned oats, pre-blended
1 packet frozen acai puree (unsweetened)
1 large frozen banana
2 cups frozen blueberries
1 cup whole milk kefir or coconut kefir
2 tablespoons almond or cashew butter
1 tablespoon honey
1 tablespoon chia seeds
1 tablespoon flax seed
½ teaspoon cinnamon

Suggested Bowl Toppings
Almond or cashew butter
Banana slices
Berries
Chia seeds
Crushed nuts
Dark chocolate shavings
Granola
Toasted coconut flakes (unsweetened)

Add all the smoothie ingredients to a blender and blend until smooth and creamy. Pour the blend into a bowl, then add toppings as desired.

To use this blend for a smoothie, skip the toppings and add ¼–½ cup of whatever liquid you like to dilute the blend to your preferred consistency for drinking. Drink the smoothie immediately, refrigerate it in an airtight container for up to 24 hours, or freeze it in an airtight container until you are ready to drink it.

Cherry–Mango Stomach Soother

Think collagen is just a beauty supplement? Think again. Thanks to amino acids, collagen can aid digestion, reduce inflammation in the gut, and even help heal stomach ulcers. This smart stomach-soothing blend combines collagen with mango, which contains fiber and polyphenols that treat constipation and gut inflammation and enzymes that help the body break down protein. In other words, this blend keeps your stomach humming the way it should!

Servings: 2–3

Ingredients:
1 packet frozen acai puree (unsweetened)
½ cup frozen mango
½ cup frozen cherries
1 cup plain or mango kefir
1 cup unsweetened coconut milk
2 tablespoons chia seeds
2 tablespoons almond butter
2 rounded tablespoons collagen powder

Add all the ingredients to a blender and blend until smooth and creamy. Drink the smoothie immediately, refrigerate it in an airtight container for up to 24 hours, or freeze it in an airtight container until you are ready to drink it.

Protein and Probiotic Powerhouse

Healthy digestion is about more than bloating and stomach upset. After all, it's your digestive system that absorbs all the powerful nutrients in these smoothie blends. If yours has been feeling a little sluggish, give this blend a try. It's full of fatty acids, soluble fiber, protein, and probiotics to keep your tummy in tip-top shape.

Servings: 2

Ingredients:
Smoothie Bowl Base
2 packets frozen acai puree (unsweetened)
2 medium frozen bananas
1 cup frozen mixed berries
½ cup low-fat plain Greek yogurt
½ cup coconut water
2 tablespoons flaxseed meal
1½ teaspoons freshly grated ginger
1 pinch kosher salt

Suggested Bowl Toppings
Chopped almonds
Drizzle of honey
Fig halves
Fresh berries
Pumpkin seeds
Unsweetened coconut flakes

Add all the smoothie ingredients to a blender and blend until smooth and creamy. Pour the blend into a bowl, then add toppings as desired.

To use this blend for a smoothie, skip the toppings and add ¼–½ cup of whatever liquid you like to dilute the blend to your preferred consistency for drinking. Drink the smoothie immediately, refrigerate it in an airtight container for up to 24 hours, or freeze it in an airtight container until you are ready to drink it.

ENERGY

Better Than Coffee

Go ahead and skip that cup of coffee. Goji berries alone can boost your mood, bring you energy, and improve your digestive health. Add some satisfying fiber and the steady energy boost of natural sugar from banana and low-glycemic berries, and you have a recipe for a great morning.

Servings: 1

Ingredients:
2 packets frozen acai puree (unsweetened)
½ medium frozen banana
¾ cup frozen mixed berries
2 tablespoons goji berries
1 tablespoon raw honey
½ cup almond milk

Add all the ingredients to a blender and blend until smooth and creamy. Drink the smoothie immediately, refrigerate it in an airtight container for up to 24 hours, or freeze it in an airtight container until you are ready to drink it.

Chocolate–Peanut Butter Blast Off

Think of this blend like a power bar in a bowl, but much tastier and more satisfying. Not only does this combination of fruit and peanut butter leave you feeling full and energized, it also makes the perfect foundation for equally nutritious-yet-delicious toppings like chopped almonds and dark chocolate. Plus, no weird processed-food aftertaste.

Servings: 1

Ingredients:
Smoothie Bowl Base
1 packet frozen acai puree (unsweetened)
1½ medium frozen bananas
½ cup frozen strawberries
½ cup frozen blueberries
¼ cup whole milk (or nondairy milk)
2 rounded tablespoons peanut butter

Suggested Bowl Toppings
Banana slices
Blueberries
Chopped almonds
Dark chocolate shavings
Peanut butter
Strawberry slices

Add all the smoothie ingredients to a blender and blend until smooth and creamy. Pour the blend into a bowl, then add toppings as desired.

To use this blend for a smoothie, skip the toppings and add ¼–½ cup of whatever liquid you like to dilute the blend to your preferred consistency for drinking. Drink the smoothie immediately, refrigerate it in an airtight container for up to 24 hours, or freeze it in an airtight container until you are ready to drink it.

Berry Energizing Workout Smoothie

Don't skip over this recipe just because you see spinach and beets! These superfoods can improve blood flow and boost your stamina while working out, and they pair beautifully with acai and mixed berries. Throw in some almond butter, with all its healthy fat, protein, and yummy nuttiness, and you have one super energizing and tasty pre-workout snack.

Servings: 1–2

Ingredients:
2 cups baby spinach leaves, pre-blended
1 packet frozen acai puree (unsweetened)
1 medium frozen banana
1½ cups frozen mixed berries
½ cup unsweetened almond milk
1 tablespoon almond butter
1 tablespoon chia seeds

Add all the ingredients to a blender and blend until smooth and creamy. Drink the smoothie immediately, refrigerate it in an airtight container for up to 24 hours, or freeze it in an airtight container until you are ready to drink it.

Strawberry-Oatmeal Stamina

Drinking this blend is like devouring a hearty bowl of oatmeal topped with fresh fruit and yogurt. And just like a hearty bowl of oatmeal, it will give you the stamina you need to slay your morning workout when you enjoy it an hour or two beforehand. (But since you'll be drinking it, remember to grind the oatmeal into a fine powder before adding the other ingredients.)

Servings: 3-4

Ingredients:
¾ cup steel-cut oats, pre-blended
1 packet frozen acai puree (unsweetened)
2 medium frozen bananas
1½ cups fresh or frozen strawberries
1 cup fresh or frozen blueberries
¾ cup plain, low-fat Greek yogurt
¼ cup unsweetened almond milk
2 teaspoons chia seeds

Add all the ingredients to a blender and blend until smooth and creamy. Drink the smoothie immediately, refrigerate it in an airtight container for up to 24 hours, or freeze it in an airtight container until you are ready to drink it.

HEART HEALTH

Blackberry-Pear Power Blend

In a world full of processing, packaging, and drive-thru windows, it can be hard to give your body the nutrients it needs to stay strong. But brightening up your diet and fortifying your heart are simple with this summery blend, which is chock-full of heart-healthy heroes like blackberries, pears, citrus, and chia seeds. If you don't love seeds in your smoothie, just press the blend through a fine-mesh strainer.

Servings: 1

Ingredients:
1 packet frozen acai puree (unsweetened)
1 medium frozen banana
2 cups frozen blackberries
1 fresh medium pear, peeled and seeded
2 teaspoons lemon juice
1 tablespoon flaxseeds
½ cup coconut water

Add all the ingredients to a blender and blend until smooth and creamy. Drink the smoothie immediately, refrigerate it in an airtight container for up to 24 hours, or freeze it in an airtight container until you are ready to drink it.

Heart Smart Smoothie

When you think of heart-healthy food, you probably picture bland vegetables and boiled fish. But with smoothies like this one, you'll never get tired of doing what's good for you! The ingredients in this blend are low in sugar and high in protein and antioxidants, helping to reduce your risk of heart disease without giving up amazing flavor.

Servings: 1

Ingredients:
Smoothie Bowl Base
2 packets frozen acai puree (unsweetened)
1 medium frozen banana
¾ cup frozen blackberries
¼ cup frozen cherries
1 small steamed and frozen beet
½ cup almond milk
1 tablespoon almond (or other nut) butter
1 scoop chocolate protein powder (optional)
1 tablespoon cacao powder (optional)

Suggested Bowl Toppings
Blackberries
Cacao nibs or dark chocolate shavings
Cherries
Chopped walnuts
Hemp seeds
Unsweetened coconut flakes

Add all the smoothie ingredients to a blender and blend until smooth and creamy. Pour the blend into a bowl, then add toppings as desired.

To use this blend for a smoothie, skip the toppings and add ¼–½ cup of whatever liquid you like to dilute the blend to your preferred consistency for drinking. Drink the smoothie immediately, refrigerate it in an airtight container for up to 24 hours, or freeze it in an airtight container until you are ready to drink it.

Blueberry Blood-Pressure Blend

Have you been warned about your high blood pressure? This is the blend for you. Antioxidants combine with potassium and probiotics in this simple but delicious blood-pressure balancing blend. Topping it off with heart-healthy pomegranate, walnuts, and dark chocolate turns "doctor's orders" into a tempting treat.

Servings: 2

Ingredients:
Smoothie Bowl Base
1 packed cup baby spinach, pre-blended
1 packet frozen acai puree (unsweetened)
1 medium frozen banana
1 cup frozen blueberries
1 cup plain, nonfat yogurt

Suggested Bowl Toppings
Banana slices
Blueberries
Chopped walnuts
Dark chocolate shavings
Pomegranate seeds

Add all the smoothie ingredients to a blender and blend until smooth and creamy. Pour the blend into a bowl, then add toppings as desired.

To use this blend for a smoothie, skip the toppings and add ¼–½ cup of whatever liquid you like to dilute the blend to your preferred consistency for drinking. Drink the smoothie immediately, refrigerate it in an airtight container for up to 24 hours, or freeze it in an airtight container until you are ready to drink it.

HYDRATION

Strawberry-Watermelon Hydration

Looking for a way to stay hydrated that's a little more exciting than water? This acai-powered blend can help with that. Watermelon and strawberries offer sweetness, antioxidants, and lots of low-calorie hydration with a water content of more than 90 percent. Throw in some coconut water for extra electrolytes and you basically have a yummy sports drink without the off-putting artificial coloring.

Servings: 1–2

Ingredients:
1 packet frozen acai puree (unsweetened)
½ medium frozen banana
1 cup frozen strawberries
1½ cups fresh watermelon cubes
Juice of 1 medium lime
½ cup coconut water
1 tablespoon chia seeds

Add all the ingredients to a blender and blend until smooth and creamy. Drink the smoothie immediately, refrigerate it in an airtight container for up to 24 hours, or freeze it in an airtight container until you are ready to drink it.

Berry-Peach Recovery Bowl

Whether you've just finished a rough sweat session or you're feeling run down from a hard week, this tasty bowl can help you bounce back. It's packed with antioxidants and electrolytes to help you rehydrate, recover, and replenish your energy stores. For the added benefits of mental recovery, take the time to savor each nourishing bite.

Servings: 1

Ingredients:
Smoothie Bowl Base
2 packets frozen acai puree (unsweetened)
1 medium frozen banana
½ cup frozen mixed berries
½ cup diced frozen peaches
½ cup coconut water

Suggested Bowl Toppings
Banana slices
Granola
Kiwi slices
Strawberry slices
Unsweetened coconut flakes
Yogurt

Add all the smoothie ingredients to a blender and blend until smooth and creamy. Pour the blend into a bowl, then add toppings as desired.

To use this blend for a smoothie, skip the toppings and add ¼–½ cup of whatever liquid you like to dilute the blend to your preferred consistency for drinking. Drink the smoothie immediately, refrigerate it in an airtight container for up to 24 hours, or freeze it in an airtight container until you are ready to drink it.

Blueberry-Lime Refresher

This is the kind of drink you imagine sipping on a front porch in the middle of summer. Except, with all the antioxidants, vitamins, minerals, and electrolytes packed into this refreshing blend, it's sure to do more for you than a sugary glass of lemonade. If you have to choose between the two on a hot day, you won't regret picking this one.

Servings: 1

Ingredients:
1 packet frozen acai puree (unsweetened)
1 cup frozen blueberries
2 sprigs mint
½ cup coconut water
Juice of 1 medium lime
1 tablespoon raw honey

Add all the ingredients to a blender and blend until smooth and creamy. Drink the smoothie immediately, refrigerate it in an airtight container for up to 24 hours, or freeze it in an airtight container until you are ready to drink it.

IMMUNE HEALTH

Immune-Boosting Smoothie

When it comes to fending off the flu, sometimes less is more—especially when just a handful of ingredients pack this much of a nutritional punch. Acai and blueberries have powerful immune-boosting properties, but almond milk brings the added benefit of anti-inflammatory vitamin E. Topped off with antioxidant-rich hemp protein powder, this blend is as effective as it is delicious.

Servings: 1–2

Ingredients:
1 packet frozen acai puree (unsweetened)
1 medium frozen banana
1 cup frozen blueberries
1½ cups almond milk
1 tablespoon hemp protein powder

Add all the ingredients to a blender and blend until smooth and creamy. Drink the blend immediately, refrigerate it in an airtight container for up to 24 hours, or freeze it in an airtight container until ready to use.

Honey-Topped Immune Health

From antioxidants to healthy fats, this blend has it all. Topping things off with honey and figs not only gives this bowl a Mediterranean feel, it also ups the immune-boosting ante. Plus, if you're already feeling a little under the weather, a bit of honey can help quell a cough.

Servings: 1

Ingredients:
Smoothie Bowl Base
1 packet frozen acai puree (unsweetened)
1 medium frozen banana
½ cup frozen blueberries
½ cup frozen strawberries
½ cup unsweetened cashew milk
1 tablespoon ground flaxseed meal

Suggested Bowl Toppings
Chia seeds
Chopped cashews or almonds
Fig halves
Fresh berries
Honey

Add all the smoothie ingredients to a blender and blend until smooth and creamy. Pour the blend into a bowl, then add toppings as desired.

To use this blend for a smoothie, skip the toppings and add ¼–½ cup of whatever liquid you like to dilute the blend to your preferred consistency for drinking. Drink the smoothie immediately, refrigerate it in an airtight container for up to 24 hours, or freeze it in an airtight container until you are ready to drink it.

Tropical Nutrition

If you're looking for a multivitamin in a smoothie bowl, this is it. (And it tastes like a tropical drink—the kind with the tiny umbrella.) The mango alone provides nearly three-quarters of the vitamin C you need in a day, not to mention 10 percent of your recommended vitamin A, which is essential for a healthy immune system. This recipe makes enough for four small servings, so that the whole family can get in on the nutrient-rich fun.

Servings: 2–4

Ingredients:
Smoothie Bowl Base
2 packets frozen acai puree (unsweetened)
2 medium frozen bananas
1½ cups frozen mango
1 cup frozen pineapple
1 cup coconut water
1–2 tablespoons lime juice

Suggested Bowl Toppings
Banana slices
Chia seeds
Chopped nuts
Kiwi slices
Strawberry slices
Unsweetened coconut flakes

Add all the smoothie ingredients to a blender and blend until smooth and creamy. Pour the blend into a bowl, then add toppings as desired.

To use this blend for a smoothie, skip the toppings and add ¼–½ cup of whatever liquid you like to dilute the blend to your preferred consistency for drinking. Drink the smoothie immediately, refrigerate it in an airtight container for up to 24 hours, or freeze it in an airtight container until you are ready to drink it.

THE ACAI BERRY MIRACLE

INFLAMMATION

Orange-Pineapple Inflammation Defense

Whether you're a weekend warrior with body aches, or you're someone who battles a painful chronic condition like arthritis, this nutrient-rich blend can help. Sweet berries and pineapple balance out the earthy flavors of kale and beet, and together, they create one amazing anti-inflammatory powerhouse of a smoothie.

Servings: 2

Ingredients:
2 cups baby kale, pre-blended
1 packet frozen acai puree (unsweetened)
1 small steamed and frozen beet
1 medium orange
2 cups frozen mixed berries
1 cup frozen pineapple
1 cup coconut water
1 tablespoon freshly grated ginger
1 tablespoon coconut oil

Add all the ingredients to a blender and blend until smooth and creamy. Drink the blend immediately, refrigerate it in an airtight container for up to 24 hours, or freeze it in an airtight container until ready to use.

Tart Cherry and Turmeric Calming Blend

More and more research ties chronic illness to inflammation, so finding new ways to combat it is essential. That's where acai blends like this one come in. This tasty recipe calls for tart cherries and turmeric, two of the most potent anti-inflammatory foods available. Keeping this blend dairy and sugar free is key to avoiding even more inflammation, so if you make any substitutions, stick to unsweetened ingredients and nondairy liquids.

Servings: 1–2

Ingredients:
1 packet frozen acai puree (unsweetened)
1 medium frozen banana
1 cup tart cherries
½ cup unsweetened coconut water
Juice of ½ medium lime
1 teaspoon turmeric

Add all the ingredients to a blender and blend until smooth and creamy. Drink the blend immediately, refrigerate it in an airtight container for up to 24 hours, or freeze it in an airtight container until ready to use.

Blueberry-Ginger Stomach Soother

Looking for a smoothie bowl packed with anti-inflammatory *and* stomach-soothing goodness? This ginger-fortified, dairy- and sugar-free blend is for you. And don't worry—you won't notice the spinach in this blend, but your body will. In addition to being generally nutritious, leafy greens contain inflammation-fighting vitamin K. Topping your bowl with chopped almonds and chia seeds provides even more anti-inflammatory benefits.

Servings: 1

Ingredients:
Smoothie Bowl Base
½ cup spinach, pre-blended
1 packet frozen acai puree (unsweetened)
1 medium frozen banana
¾ cup frozen blueberries
½ cup unsweetened almond milk
1 teaspoon freshly minced ginger (or ½ teaspoon ground ginger)
1 tablespoon almond butter
1 tablespoon ground flaxseed meal
1 scoop vanilla protein powder (optional)

Suggested Bowl Toppings
Almond butter
Chia seeds
Chopped almonds
Fresh berries
Peaches
Unsweetened coconut flakes

Add all the smoothie ingredients to a blender and blend until smooth and creamy. Pour the blend into a bowl, then add toppings as desired.

To use this blend for a smoothie, skip the toppings and add ¼–½ cup of whatever liquid you like to dilute the blend to your preferred consistency for drinking. Drink the smoothie immediately, refrigerate it in an airtight container for up to 24 hours, or freeze it in an airtight container until you are ready to drink it.

MOOD

Easy Does It

When you're feeling overwhelmed, the last thing you need is a complicated recipe first thing in the morning. That's why this blend keeps it simple with just a handful of mood-boosting ingredients. And remember, the very act of eating a nutritious breakfast has been shown to improve your mood, so you're already ahead of the game!

Servings: 1

Ingredients:
Smoothie Bowl Base
1 packed cup baby spinach, pre-blended
1 packet frozen acai puree (unsweetened)
1 medium frozen banana
1 cup frozen mixed berries
½ cup unsweetened vanilla almond milk

Suggested Bowl Toppings
Banana slices
Chopped nuts
Dark chocolate shavings
Fresh berries
Unsweetened coconut flakes

Add all the smoothie ingredients to a blender and blend until smooth and creamy. Pour the blend into a bowl, then add toppings as desired.

To use this blend for a smoothie, skip the toppings and add ¼–½ cup of whatever liquid you like to dilute the blend to your preferred consistency for drinking. Drink the smoothie immediately, refrigerate it in an airtight container for up to 24 hours, or freeze it in an airtight container until you are ready to drink it.

Everything Good

Think of this blend as a mood-boosting medicinal cocktail. Every one of the ingredients contributes to your happiness, whether it's through energizing B vitamins, antidepressive probiotics, or several other uplifting nutrients. Although it's not a magic wand, a cup full of nutritional goodness can only help.

Servings: 3–4

Ingredients:
½ packed cup baby spinach, pre-blended
¾ cup steel-cut oats, pre-blended
1 packet frozen acai puree (unsweetened)
1 medium frozen banana
¼ medium avocado
2 cups fresh or frozen blueberries
¾ cup plain, low-fat Greek yogurt
¼ cup unsweetened almond milk
2 teaspoons chia seeds

Add all the ingredients to a blender and blend until smooth and creamy. Drink the smoothie immediately, refrigerate it in an airtight container for up to 24 hours, or freeze it in an airtight container until you are ready to drink it.

Banana-Berry Mood Booster

Have you ever noticed how rundown you feel after a busy week filled with drive-thru windows and takeout containers? It may not be your workload making you feel that way. Your brain needs the nutrients found in whole, healthful foods just as much as your body does. That's where this acai-powered blend comes in. From antioxidants to omega-3 fatty acids, this smoothie bowl has what your brain needs to lift you out of that stressful space.

Servings: 1

Ingredients:
Smoothie Bowl Base
1 packet frozen acai puree (unsweetened)
1 medium frozen banana
¼ cup dried goji berries
½ cup frozen strawberries
¼ cup almond milk
½ teaspoon vanilla extract
1 tablespoon hemp seeds

Suggested Bowl Toppings
Chia seeds
Chopped nuts
Fig halves
Fresh berries
Unsweetened coconut flakes

Add all the smoothie ingredients to a blender and blend until smooth and creamy. Pour the blend into a bowl, then add toppings as desired.

To use this blend for a smoothie, skip the toppings and add ¼–½ cup of whatever liquid you like to dilute the blend to your preferred consistency for drinking. Drink the smoothie immediately, refrigerate it in an airtight container for up to 24 hours, or freeze it in an airtight container until you are ready to drink it.

WEIGHT LOSS

Skinny Strawberry-Grapefruit Smoothie

One of the easiest ways to slim down your smoothies is to replace milk with unsweetened fruit juice. This blend uses grapefruit, which studies show can be helpful in losing weight because it helps you feel full. Combine that with the energy and soluble fiber from berries, and you have the perfect afternoon snack.

Servings: 1

Ingredients:
1 packet frozen acai puree (unsweetened)
1 medium frozen banana
¾ cup fresh or frozen blueberries
½ cup fresh or frozen strawberries
½ cup grapefruit juice

Add all the ingredients to a blender and blend until smooth and creamy. Drink the smoothie immediately, refrigerate it in an airtight container for up to 24 hours, or freeze it in an airtight container until you are ready to drink it.

Avocado-Citrus All-Star

When you're trying to lose weight, it's easy to lose sight of the real goal: feeling good about yourself. This low-glycemic bowl, with all of its hydration and fiber, can help you not only get a step closer to that goal but also feel great along the way. In addition to helping you maintain a healthy weight, these yummy ingredients may lower your blood pressure and cholesterol, balance your blood sugar, improve your digestion, and fight inflammation.

Servings: 1

Ingredients:
Smoothie Bowl Base
1 packet frozen acai puree (unsweetened)
1 medium frozen banana
½ cup frozen strawberries
½ medium avocado
½ cup orange sections
½ cup coconut water

Suggested Bowl Toppings
Chia seeds
Chopped almonds
Kiwi slices
Strawberry slices
Sunflower seeds

Add all the smoothie ingredients to a blender and blend until smooth and creamy. Pour the blend into a bowl, then add toppings as desired.

To use this blend for a smoothie, skip the toppings and add ¼–½ cup of whatever liquid you like to dilute the blend to your preferred consistency for drinking. Drink the smoothie immediately, refrigerate it in an airtight container for up to 24 hours, or freeze it in an airtight container until you are ready to drink it.

Cherry-Berry Morning Fuel

You won't find a better way to start your day than with an acai bowl full of healthful, energizing ingredients. Natural sugars and soluble fiber give you a buzz that lasts longer than coffee's while the antioxidant and anti-inflammatory properties go to work on your overall wellness. (This bowl also packs an immune-boosting punch, which makes it perfect for enjoying before heading to work.)

Servings: 1

Ingredients:
Smoothie Bowl Base
½ cup spinach or kale, pre-blended
1 packet frozen acai puree (unsweetened)
1 medium frozen banana
1½ cups frozen mixed berries
¼ cup fresh or frozen cherries
½ tablespoon ground flaxseed meal
Juice of ½ medium lemon
½ cup coconut water
1 pinch turmeric (optional)

Suggested Bowl Toppings
Banana slices
Chia seeds
Chopped nuts
Fresh berries
Unsweetened coconut flakes

Add all the smoothie ingredients to a blender and blend until smooth and creamy. Pour the blend into a bowl, then add toppings as desired.

To use this blend for a smoothie, skip the toppings and add ¼–½ cup of whatever liquid you like to dilute the blend to your preferred consistency for drinking. Drink the smoothie immediately, refrigerate it in an airtight container for up to 24 hours, or freeze it in an airtight container until you are ready to drink it.

Happy Body Bowl

Is it dessert? Or is it health food? Your taste buds won't be able to tell, but your body will definitely notice a difference! Mango is the shining star of this show, benefiting almost every aspect of your wellness while tasting amazing, but every ingredient adds essential nutrients (even the maple syrup!). Work this bowl into your weekly routine for a happy body.

Servings: 1–2

Ingredients:
Smoothie Bowl Base
1 cup baby spinach, pre-blended
1 packet frozen acai puree (unsweetened)
1 small frozen banana
1 cup frozen mango
¼ medium avocado
¼ cup almond milk
¼ cup water
1 tablespoon ground flaxseed meal
1–2 teaspoons maple syrup (optional)

Suggested Bowl Toppings
Banana slices
Cacao nibs or dark chocolate shavings
Cashew butter
Ground cinnamon
Low-fat granola
Mango slices

Add all the smoothie ingredients to a blender and blend until smooth and creamy. Pour the blend into a bowl, then add toppings as desired.

To use this blend for a smoothie, skip the toppings and add ¼–½ cup of whatever liquid you like to dilute the blend to your preferred consistency for drinking. Drink the smoothie immediately, refrigerate it in an airtight container for up to 24 hours, or freeze it in an airtight container until you are ready to drink it.

Blackberry Magic

If you're looking for a simple smoothie blend that will still work wonders for your overall health, this is it. Blackberries offer more than enough nutrients to keep your body in tip-top shape. They contain vitamin C to battle free radicals (and head colds), fiber to reduce cholesterol and improve gut health, vitamin K for blood clotting, manganese for bone health and a strong immune system, and antioxidants for brain health. Oh, and they taste amazing!

Servings: 1

Ingredients:
1 packet frozen acai puree (unsweetened)
1 medium frozen banana
1 cup frozen blackberries
½ cup almond milk
½ teaspoon ground cinnamon
2 tablespoons ground flaxseed meal

Add all the ingredients to a blender and blend until smooth and creamy. Drink the smoothie immediately, refrigerate it in an airtight container for up to 24 hours, or freeze it in an airtight container until you are ready to drink it.

Pumpkin Spice Powerhouse

This final recipe teaches you to think outside the box. When it comes to acai bowls, there are no rules and no limits. So why not pumpkin pie? After all, pumpkin is more than just a fall flavor. It's rich in antioxidants, vitamin A, vitamin C, potassium, and fiber. This blend combines it with nutrient-rich papaya and pie spices for a bowl that will knock your socks off.

Servings: 1

Ingredients:
Smoothie Bowl Base
1 packet frozen acai puree (unsweetened)
⅔ medium frozen banana
½ cup frozen papaya
½ can organic pumpkin
1 cup almond milk
1 tablespoon maca
1 tablespoon ground cinnamon
1 tablespoon pumpkin pie spice

Suggested Bowl Toppings
Banana slices
Chopped nuts
Low-fat granola
Papaya slices
Pomegranate seeds

Add all the smoothie ingredients to a blender and blend until smooth and creamy. Pour the blend into a bowl, then add toppings as desired.

To use this blend for a smoothie, skip the toppings and add ¼–½ cup of whatever liquid you like to dilute the blend to your preferred consistency for drinking. Drink the smoothie immediately, refrigerate it in an airtight container for up to 24 hours, or freeze it in an airtight container until you are ready to drink it.

ABOUT THE AUTHOR

Annie Willis is passionate about health and wellness. After years of poor health and exhaustion, she found relief in whole, healthy foods and fell in love with preparing them at home. Annie lives in Colorado with her husband and their two Pomeranians, Olive and Basil.

MORE FROM SKYHORSE PUBLISHING!

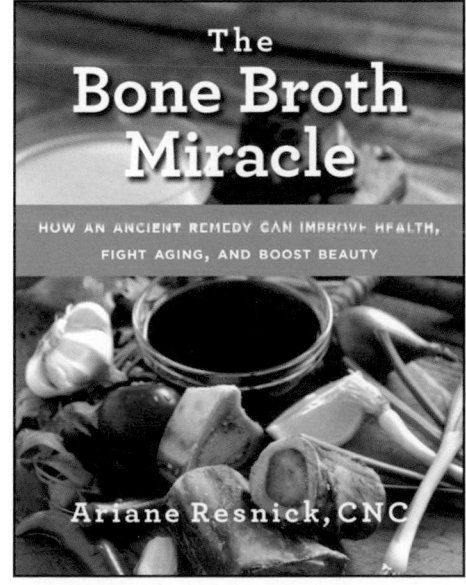